Footpaths & Fishing Boats

Growing up in Nipper's Harbour

Audrey Starkes

This book is dedicated to my father, Ward Starkes,

who set sail from this life on October 25, 1998.

Acknowledgements

I would like to thank all the people of Nipper's Harbour, living and dead, who were there when I was growing up. You made me who I am, and were the inspiration for this book.

I would like especially to acknowledge my Mother, Stella Starkes, who encouraged me every step of the way, listened to all my stories and helped me tweak some details.

Thanks to Susan Jennings, who told me I could write and got me started on this journey, and to my fellow writers of The Ottawa Story Spinners. Thanks also to my friends who have encouraged me, listened to me, and nudged me along the path to the completion of this work.

To my editors at Petra Books, Peter Geldart and Danielle Aubrey, thank you for your patience, design work and enhancement of my stories with your fresh perspective.

To my uncle who reviewed my manuscript and made many useful suggestions. Please note that special Newfoundland dialect words are in **bold**, and can be found defined in the glossary.

And finally, to my partner, Edith Moore, who listened to every version of every story over and over, and kept me 'steady as she goes'.

Preface

In 2004 I attended a landmark celebration in Nipper's Harbour. It was the 200th anniversary of the settlement, and my ancestors were one of the founding families. A lot of the activities took place in Welsh's Cove. I was flooded with memories of Sunday School picnics. I renewed acquaintances, saw people from the distant past, met people who had left before I was born, and heard marvellous yarns. On the Saturday morning of that anniversary weekend, I was having breakfast at the Community Hall and found myself chatting with a gentleman who fell into the category of having left Nipper's Harbour before I was born. But he shared my enthusiasm for the energy in the place, and it soon became clear that even though we had grown up in different eras, we had been shaped by the same elements. It was one of those never-to-be-forgotten contacts. His name was Pastor Earl Batstone, a retired official in the Pentecostal Assemblies of Newfoundland. He told me about his family – his mother, his sisters – and growing up in Batstone's Cove. He also told me how he and his buddies invented a "flying machine" when they were kids, and had it all set to go from atop the "Blowing Hole" – the mount of the 72 steps – but alas, it failed!

He drew me a picture of it. I was struck by the details, and the fact that he told the story with such joy and abandonment. It inspired me, and stirred me to write my own stories.

Years later I was informed that Earl had "crossed over". I regret that I did not get to share my written stories with him, because he was keenly interested in anything that had to do with Nipper's Harbour.

Table of Contents

Introduction

*Sitting in the motorboat at the Union Store wharf, the boat rocking and people jumping about. The smell of gasoline as the motor started, dried fish scales on the **tawts**, as we settled down for the ride to the cove. My Mom digging around in the purchases she had made, and producing club sandwiches – a confection that I suspect had come from the U.K., perhaps from Tunnocks of Scotland. Wrapped in waxed paper with blue printing on it – almost like the wrapping on the Red Delicious apples just before Christmas. The unwrapped product revealed a pink wafer sandwich with thick marshmallow inside. The sides were dipped in chocolate and coconut. I was hooked after my first bite. I might have become a club-sandwich addict, had those bars been available all the time. But they weren't. An occasional shipment, snapped up in no time.*

I ate them methodically. First, I carefully ate those chocolate coconut sides in delicate little nibbles, then squished the pink wafers to make the marshmallow spill out the sides and ate the marshmallow. Lastly, the pink wafers. It was divine.

These images are clear as a bell. They flood back to me at will, with little or no effort. I thought everyone remembered this way, but now realize this is a gift. Who knew?

The clarity of the aforementioned vignette is the clarity found in all the stories in this collection and then some. My experiences shaped who I am. They are embedded in my soul. They inform my heart. They nourish my essence. They are the building blocks to my authentic self.

The stories are written from the heart of the child within, the place where all truth is found. I believe that distancing and disconnectedness from that source is the cause of much sorrow.

Although I physically left Nipper's Harbour a long time ago, it has always remained with me. I go to New-foundland each year, and always go to Nipper's Harbour. Without fail, I go to the Lookout.

It is my hope that those who read these accounts of life in Nipper's Harbour before the road will con-nect with their own experiences of an earlier life, and in so doing gain a deeper appreciation of their roots and connection with their beginnings. For people who grew up in Newfoundland and especially in Nipper's Harbour, I hope you will be able to relive some of the images. You might have experienced them differently, and it's your experience that counts. It has been noteworthy that people who do not have Newfoundland roots have reported a connection to their own childhoods when I have read these stories. I have appreciated this feedback as it has affirmed the metaphorical depth and intent of what might be seen at first glance as simply manifest storytelling. Whether or not you were born in Nipper's Harbour or grew up there, I hope my stories will move you. I hope they make you laugh and make you cry. I hope they touch the human place in your heart that will help you appreciate each person you meet as a unique, important individual. I hope they make you pay attention to yourself and help you honour your heart.

Footpaths & Fishing Boats

A Fisherman's Daughter

I remember the days before fish-processing plants, when all the fish were preserved in salt, and stored in barrels to be shipped off mostly to Europe and the West Indies. My Dad and his brothers, Uncle Cyril and Uncle Ralph, and their fishing partner, Frank, worked late into the night during the busy period. They gutted, salted and packed, mostly codfish, immediately after it was caught in order to preserve the quality of the fish. Other species of fish were preserved in this way too: salmon, turbot, herring and mackerel. There was no electricity in the **stages**. Oil lamps hung from the rafters in those splitting rooms in the stages, attached to the wharves where the boats were tied or moored. There was a hole in the floor where the fish guts were thrown and disposed of — washed out to sea to be recycled — maybe a feed of sushi for the porpoises and whales that danced around the ocean in the summer. The liver was placed in separate barrels, which sat in the sun to **render**. Yes, a big market for that. That smell was so pungent and over-powering that I routinely held my breath as I passed the barrels on the way to the wharf. Hard to believe that cod liver oil is good for you.

While much of the codfish was salted and stored in barrels (referred to as *salt bulk fish*) some of it was salted and dried on **flakes**. This drying process was largely the women's department. A **fish flake** is not an easy thing to describe, an open platform which also allowed air circulation from the bottom. Loose slender poles aided in this openness, which was fantastic for drying the fish but tricky for the humans spreading the cod. When the sun shone, the women ran to the flakes to spread the fish and maximize the benefits of the sunlight. But the minute a rain cloud appeared they raced to gather the fish in piles over which they placed a tent-like clapboard wooden structure called a **fish-cover** to keep it dry.

That's what we ate in the winter — salt cod. Salt fish and potatoes, salt fish and **brewis**‡, salt fish and

---

‡ *To the uninitiated, brewis can look and taste a bit daunting. A friend of mine from Montreal called it "soaked cardboard". The blandness of brewis was livened up with scrunchions, known in Quebec as "lardons". It's fat pork (pork belly), diced and fried. The Italians call it "pancetta" — a snobby version of scrunchions or lardons.*

homemade bread. Salt everything, come to think of it. The only refrigeration in those days was the Bait Depot, which had its own generator that ran 24/7. This is where fishermen stored bait for their **trawls** — squid, caplin, sometimes herring. But meat, such as beef or lamb, could also be stored there. Sometimes my parents bought a quarter of beef from beef farmers in a more pastoral area of Newfoundland (Nipper's Harbour was bald rugged rock) and stored it in the depot. But salt beef and salt pork also comprised a sizable portion of our diet.

The codfish was caught in **traps** and on trawls. A cod-trap is big, and optimally requires two motorboats and a dory to haul a large three-dimensional net. The fish are alive in the trap and dipped out with a large **dip-net** into the waiting skiff. The trawls were placed in deeper water because they went out in a long line many fathoms into the ocean, with a short line and hook attached at regular intervals. Turbot was frequently caught on trawls, but also codfish. Salmon, herring and mackerel had their own specific nets with specific mesh sizes. And the fishermen, including my Dad and his family made their own nets.

The nets were made mostly in the net house. On the Starkes' family property, along with the potato garden and the storehouse, was the net house. This was a two-story structure, where you went from the bottom floor to the top floor via a ladder, although there was an outside door too that you could access via a precarious bridge. Inside there was a woodstove, because in the winter the men spent most days in the net house, mending nets and making nets. Some nets such as caplin seines were made at the family home.

The most basic style of catching cod was in a small boat such as a dory with a jigger. A jigger was a heavy sinker and hook attached to a long fishing line that was wound around a wooden frame made for that purpose. Even as a little girl I was allowed to cod-jig. You let out the fishing line until it hit bottom, then reeled in three fathoms of fishing line, and held it in place. Then simply pulled the line back and forth until you felt a bite. Codfish that were jigged or caught in the **cod-trap** were the most delicious. They were caught in more shallow water than the codfish that had been caught on a **trawl**. And the jigging was done mostly for domestic eating purposes, including what was salted for us to eat in the winter.

The fish my Mom cooked was the most delicious I have ever had. Barely out of the ocean it was cleaned and brought home and cooked immediately. Codfish, cod tongues and salmon were my favourites. All summer long we ate, and ate, and ate all we wanted. It was supremely abundant. And the salted varieties in the winter had their own deliciousness. Coming home from school to the smell of salt cod, **brewis** and scrunchions just warmed the cockles of my heart.

Fishing has changed in Newfoundland. The last twenty years of my Dad's career was in a long-liner. Away from home for days and weeks at a time, they fished with gillnets for cod, with crab as a by-catch for which there was no market in those days. They sold their catch to a fish processing plant.

I'm a fish and seafood snob – a genuine one. I can tell the quality of any fish mostly by looking at it. In my opinion the only place to get quality fresh fish and seafood in Ottawa is at Lapointe's in the Byward Market. I stand in amazement at the fish counter in supermarkets and watch unsuspecting landlubbers who have never clapped eyes on the ocean, pointing at slimy filets of sole. And I suppress the urge to say, "You don't really want that". Or marinated filets of anything – often catfish. Dead giveaway. They're masking the staleness of whatever it is they're marinating.

*Fish smells. There's the smell of fresh fish and the smell of stale fish. It is this discernment that contributes to my snobbery. When I walk into Lapointe's, the smell takes me back to my childhood, hanging around the fishing **stages** and wharves in Nipper's Harbour.*

Sometimes I just go into Lapointe's to absorb the atmosphere and take in the visuals and odours. I feel like I've come home. It's hard to leave without purchasing something, even if it's just a few Newfoundland smoked caplin from the refrigerator section.

When I went home for visits, there was always fresh cooked crabmeat. Sometimes I came back to Montreal, or Toronto, or Windsor, or Ottawa (wherever I was living at the time) with jars of preserved crabmeat. And smugly go off to class or work with crab salad sandwiches for lunch.

Now I make do with the best fish I'm able to get in a land-locked environment. Fish and seafood comprise about 60% of the protein I eat. I've developed a taste for pickerel, a lake fish, and was indulged by a work colleague in my last position before retirement. She and her husband would drive way, way north on the Ottawa River a couple of times a year and fly fish for pickerel. After one of Sue and Peter's fishing expeditions, I would come into work and Sue would say, "Check the freezer section in the fridge in the kitchen". Inside, frozen in water, would be filets of pickerel. This was a joyful experience!

One Christmas when my parents were visiting Ottawa, I foolishly bought trout at Loblaw's – Pretoria Bridge, touted to have a good fish monger. On Christmas Eve, as tradition dictated, we were going to have fish for dinner. The trout was placed in a proper fish steamer with lemon and dill and I turned it on. We were going to the 7:00 PM family service on Christmas Eve so fortunately had planned to eat early. All of a sudden the smell of the cooking fish began to circulate. I was a bit suspicious and then looked at my Dad sitting in the living room – his nose was poised and slightly wrinkled with a quizzical expression on his face. "Dad", I said, "that fish isn't fresh, is it?" "No", he said.

I called the fish monger at Loblaws and presented my plight. "Come right over," he said, which I did fifteen minutes before closing and he presented me with six salmon filets, decently fresh, which we had for dinner.

I had my first bone-density test a couple of years ago. The doctor said I have amazing bones. I smiled to myself, thinking probably all that fish I've eaten over the years, to say nothing of all those hills I've climbed in Nipper's Harbour probably created this optimal state of bones. A fisherman's daughter, for sure.

Grandma Starkes'

It was a wood-frame two-story house on the upper part of Starkes' **Room**. It was on top of a hill and from the back door you could look down into Randall's Cove, where there was another wood-frame two-story house built into a cliff and a small wharf nearby. There was a wooden fence around Grandma Starkes' house, and access to the garden was via two gates at opposite sides. Up on the left was yet another mound where there were an assortment of houses: the hen house, the sheep's house and an outhouse. Beside the back door was a rope-swing structure that my Grandfather had built for me. He was a fine carpenter. He was a fine man. He used to say I was a great girl, and Grandma called me her little dear. I was their first grandchild.

My Great Grandmother lived with them, and also my Dad's youngest brother and his wife. My Dad's oldest brother lived there until he got married which was when I was 7 or 8 years old. My Great Grandmother who lived well into her 90s, had a rocking chair near the wood stove in the kitchen. She was wiry and agile. She had long grey hair that she braided and wore in a bun. She wore navy-blue dresses and laced-up old-lady black oxford shoes. She was cheerful. She smiled and chuckled, and didn't have teeth. Actually, she had one bottom tooth, a long one in the middle that she played with with her tongue. Her bedroom was at the top of the stairs — it was a large one with two windows, making it bright. Great Grandmother read newspapers and Sunday School papers in her rocking chair — she mouthed the words and whispered aloud as she read. Before I went home after a visit I had to go around and hug and kiss everybody. Everyone was quite huggable but I used to be cautious of Great Grandmother, because she was bony, and along with her sunken mouth, had stray whiskers that stabbed you quite sharply when you kissed her. No matter which angle you kissed her from you'd get stabbed. But she loved me. On my fifth birthday she gave me a small heart-shaped gold locket that I still have.

Great Grandmother would plan an outing to visit her son, my Great Uncle Fred, who also lived on Starkes' **Room**. When she went out, she donned a navy-blue coat and a navy-blue tam. She wore a navy-blue dress when she died suddenly on the day of our

Sunday-school picnic in 1961. But that's another story.

The back porch leading to my Grandparents' house was long and enclosed. I suspect it was built to protect the house from the howling winds upon that hill. The windows rattled and whistled as the winds blew. I used to love the sound, and the feeling of security and protection as I nestled in the kitchen. There was a washbasin in the porch off the kitchen. Soap and towels and a jug of water were nearby. This is where the men washed up before dinner, after they came home from fishing.

The kitchen had a bracket and lamp on the wall and next to it was an ornate picture with the inscription that read:

> Christ is the head of this house
> The unseen guest at every meal
> The silent listener to every conversation.

I wasn't very old when I could read this, and being quite literal in my interpretation, it fed my wild imagination. I had visions of God and the angels jammed into Grandma's kitchen reading all our minds, judging our intentions, and keeping us all in line.

There was a trap door in the kitchen floor. Somebody (any one of the available adults) would hang onto me when that trap door was opened, which just fed my curiosity. But my Grandmother, a worrier, lived in eternal dread that something terrible would happen to me — i.e. fall in the cellar, so I never got to look into the hole. Instead, I would observe Aunt Mabel disappear into the floor, and a few minutes later, her hand would appear, placing a mason jar on the floor. Then it would disappear again, and perhaps the next time her whole body would emerge, carrying another mason jar in her hand. These jars held preserves such as blueberries, pickles or jam. Then the trap door was replaced and I was released from whosever grip I was in.

Off the kitchen was a pantry, where there were cupboards and a sink to wash dishes; and off the pantry was a smaller closet where food was stored — dried fruit, nutmeg and nutmeg grinder, canned goods, etc. The pantry was where the women gossiped, talking in whispers, as they cleaned the dishes. It really bothered me that I couldn't hear what they were saying. I recall staring at the ends of their aprons, hanging onto their legs and straining to hear. And feeling sort of cranky that I wasn't included in this conspiracy.

The parlour was infrequently used before the days of electricity and television, but occasionally, if there were special guests, we sat in there. I recall there were an over-stuffed brocade burgundy sofa and chair, and an ornate pump organ and stool, which spun around to accommodate the height of the person playing. The room had a faint musty odour, due partly to infrequent use, as well as the fact there was no central heating. There was a certain decorum expected in the parlour, which contrasted with the informality of the kitchen. It was a bit like going to church, where you had to sit and behave yourself. After Great Grandmother died and was laid out in there, I always felt a bit uneasy. I would rather not go in there, truth be known, especially if suddenly everyone left the room, and I found myself there by myself. It didn't take me long to leave.

Downstairs, across the hall from the parlour was my Grandparents' bedroom. Although we had indoor plumbing as far back as I can remember, my Grandparents did not have this installed until later. So when I needed the washroom, I was taken to that bedroom, where there was an ornate earthen chamber pot underneath the bed. There was a floral design on the front. The chamber pots were emptied into a tall enamel pail with a lid each day and its contents disposed of in the outhouse.

Meanwhile, Grandma's bedroom held other fascinations for me. Not only did I get to squat on the earthen chamber pot, but afterwards played at the dresser for a while. There was a small wooden vanity stool that pulled up to the dresser. On it was a brush, comb and mirror set — gilded and ornate — and perfumes. I would sometimes help myself to a dab of this or that, and when I returned to the kitchen the adults would chuckle. It was a mystery to me, how they knew I had been into the perfume bottles, oblivious to the extent I had doused myself.

Upstairs, next to Great Grandmother's inner sanctum, was my Uncle Cyril's room. He taught me to write before I went to school, so I assumed I had *carte blanche* access to any and all of his writing materials. I knew which drawer had the writing paper and helped myself. I wrote and drew pictures, and put it back when I was finished. When he went to write a letter, he would be confronted with my latest works. I still have the last letter he wrote to me in 1983, just a short while before his death.

I learned to knit at Grandma's house, with real yarn, from the wool of the sheep my Grandfather kept. She made me learn and practice with raw grey wool, and after I stopped dropping masses of stitches and making a general mess of things, she graduated me to green wool. It felt like I had earned my PhD in knitting.

Grandpa took me with him to tend the sheep, and I was allowed to feed the chickens from a very young age. There are many photographs of me as a pre-schooler surrounded by chickens, with a bowl of chicken feed in my hands, which I'm sprinkling about. Every time I use my *Fitz and Floyd Rooster* salt and pepper shakers, I smile and remember.

After we had fed the chickens and the sheep, sometimes Grandpa took me with him to the Lookout. He brought the binoculars and in his pocket had a few peppermint knobs. On a sunny day there was often a breeze, and he was careful to hold my hand until we got to my little carved-out seat in the rock face where I sat. He had large freckled hands with brown age spots. He would stand and look through the binoculars until he spotted my Dad and his brothers at the **cod-trap**, and then he would let me look. After that we had a peppermint knob, and he would take me by the hand until we got back to the house.

I'm quite partial to lamb's wool. On cold winter days in Ottawa, I wear red lamb's wool socks in my boots to stay warm. And in my great collection of mittens, I have a pair of grey trigger mitts toted back from my annual pilgrimage to Newfoundland. And a knitted salt and pepper hat. My attachment to these items has deep roots.

And on nights when I can't sleep, I'll think of the wind in the porch at my Grandparents' house, or go to the Lookout with my Grandpa, and know that I am safe and all is well.

Dance of the Seasons

I f I had the gift of music, I would write a symphony of the seasons as they unfolded in Nipper's Harbour that would rival Vivaldi's Four Seasons.

I shall start with Spring. The smell of fresh tar for the boats. The sound of hammers. The sight of seal's blood on freshly-fallen Spring snow. All the senses were awakened from the hypnotic survival routines of winter. All signals to us children that we were commencing the last stretch to summer break from school.

On the beach men lit fires and cooked up large vats of Patent bark resin in which fishing nets were immersed and then laid out to dry. Fresh tar was applied to the bottoms of overturned boats, which had been shrouded in tarpaulins to protect them from the harsh winter elements. The tap-tap of caulking, the hammering in place of loosened **tawts,** or ensuring the secure spots for **tole** pins on the gunwales went on in enthusiastic rhythm.

Inside the houses, women organized their Spring cleaning. As the temperatures started to climb a bit, blankets were weaned off the beds in layers, their laundering displayed on clotheslines. A good breeze and sunshine were needed for quilts. Breezes were abundant, but not sunshine. Those opportunities had to be grabbed. A dermatologist once asked me if I had had bad sunburns as a child. I responded that I hadn't had sun as a child, never mind sunburns. The natural UV protection of fog and mist.

As the snow melted, the steps on the hills emerged from their hibernation. During the winter Clifford would have shovelled them. If he had ever been examined he would probably have been diagnosed with hebephrenic schizophrenia (given his laughing, uncontrollable outbursts of giggling, mumbling to himself, and repetitive speech). But there was no need for labelling in Nipper's Harbour. Clifford was given, and did, meaningful work. With the disappearance of snow, came the rivulets of running water underneath the steps and the growth of underbrush, stinging nettles, dandelions and other signs of life.

I begged my Mother to let me wear my shoes as soon as a bit of earth emerged through the snow banks. She, and other mothers had this silly notion that you couldn't wear shoes until the snow was all gone and things had dried up. The boots were kept close at hand until June because you never knew when a Spring batch of snow would fall.

Seal meat was the featured cuisine in the Spring. Men went into treacherous iceberg-laden waters to hunt seals, used not only for food, but the pelts meant extra income from the then-popular seal industry. It was a short-lived, focused activity before the beginning of the salmon and cod fishery season.

As the final days of the school year concluded, the anticipation of summer was heightened. It was tradition that on the last day of school we had a picnic. We hiked to the bottom of the harbour, which involved a winding trail through rough terrain. At the end was a lovely grassy meadow and waterfalls. We played games and had our picnic lunch and hiked home. Never mind that we were bone weary and full of mosquito bites — on Monday morning we did not have to get up for school. And the rhythm of summer would begin.

Six days of the week, around 3:00 AM, I would awaken to the sound of a boiling kettle. Realizing it was my Dad getting ready to leave, I'd drift off to sleep again. He would eat a small meal, and after I was up and had eaten my breakfast, he would be back from the first haul, and have another breakfast. But as I would be drifting off to sleep after his first breakfast I would be aware of the put-put of motorboat engines, as boats unmoored and set off for the early morning hauls.

My bedroom window faced a back pebble stone lane. The window was raised with the screen in the summer, making me privy to early morning conversations between two fishermen who lived up the lane. Sheep rattled around on those pebble stones too, baaing and carrying on. One morning I overheard this exchange between the two fishermen:

Carl: *"Look at dem ole sheep Ches **b'y**,*
   eatin' the stingers.
    Why do day eat dem I wonder?"
Ches: *"I don't know **b'y**.*
    'Tis a rayleesh I spose."

I lay in bed, giggling away to myself, thinking about the sheep in search of a relish, perhaps needing something with more of a bite than boring old grass.

Summer was action-packed. The men were constantly busy, coming and going to the fishing nets and the women were always trying to time the meals — not easy with the unpredictability of the schedule. Winds, tides, and size of the catch were all determining variables in the fishing timetable. Our front porch with a screen door faced the main road in the cove. When I wasn't prowling around with my school friends Nancy and Shirley, I sat on the daybed in that front porch and watched everything that was going on. It was my spy couch. And there was lots going on. Within my field of vision was the door to Aunt Alma's shop, which was attached to their house. When anyone entered the shop a bell rang, signalling to Aunt Alma that her service was needed. So she stopped whatever she was doing in the house and ran out to the store. If Nanc went in the shop door instead of the back door to their house, she yelled "Me, Mom!" so her mother wouldn't have to come out. Nanc yelled "Me, Mom!" all summer long as she went in and out many times a day.

Uncle Lo, Aunt Alma's husband, and a fisherman, went in and out too but always used the back door; he didn't use the door to the shop. Their black cocker spaniel, Chub (short for Chubby) barked his head off every time someone walked by the fence. Uncle Lo was always in a hurry, and muttering to himself. *"Dyin' jumpin' reevin' screechin"* was his favourite expression of displeasure and it was said with great emphasis.

The people who went into Aunt Alma's shop were usually women from the cove who needed something to put into a recipe, or an excuse to get out of the house and see what was going on. Sometimes there were visitors from Away staying with relatives in the cove. There was one woman from New York, whose sister lived in the cove, and who came to visit several summers. She was all glammed up with ornate costume jewellery and fancy clothes. I preferred the view from my spy couch, but one day I got caught in Aunt Alma's shop when this woman came in. I suppose in an attempt to be friendly, she signalled to me that my fly zipper was down. She actually came over, touched my fly zipper and said in a friendly attempt to be Newfie *"Your zipper is down maid."* I was embarrassed, mortified, insulted and felt that the pompous woman from Away had a thing or two to learn about boundaries and protocol. I reported the whole transaction to my Mother, who kept a poker face as she listened and had the good sense not to laugh.

Aunt Alma's shop was close to the beach, where some people emptied their pails (the ones that contained the contents of the chamber pots). Women who lived up that pebble stone lane where my bedroom window faced walked down that lane with their pails to heave into the Atlantic Ocean. On their way back they often dropped into Aunt Alma's shop to buy something. They would park their pails outside the door of the shop, and pick them up on the way out. I could tell who was in the shop from my spy couch by the size, shape and colour of the rim of each pail. Sometimes there would be 3 or 4 pails — the parking lot would be almost full!

After leaving Aunt Alma's shop, one of them might drop in for a visit with my Mom, in which case they parked the pail on our back porch, so I could tell who was in the house if I happened to be returning from one of my prowls.

Thus, I lolly-gagged away the summer — playing with my impressive collection of dolls, reading, colouring and observing from my spy-couch on rainy days. Out tearing around with Nanc and Shirl on fine days. Before you knew it, summer was gone. It was time to get your clothes and school materials together and prepare for the new teacher.

The official transitioning day to Fall was Labour Day. That's the day we went on a major berry-picking expedition. Usually we went in convoy in boats with friends or family. We had buckets and jugs and containers of all descriptions, and food, including food for a cook-up at the end of the day on the beach. Sometimes we went to Burton's Pond, often to Rogue's Harbour after the last family had moved out of there and re-located to Nipper's Harbour. Rogue's Harbour was interesting because in addition to wild berries, there was an abundance of gooseberry bushes down near the beach. They were tricky to pick because of the thorns, but made delicious jam. And up the hill hidden away in the over-growth was an old abandoned well. One year, my Uncle who was visiting from Toronto fell down that well — two nano-seconds after my Mother had yelled a sharp and clear warning *"Be careful Raymond — there's an old well up that hill."* The timing was the stuff sit-coms are made of.

Labour Day was great because there were lots of us all together, and it triggered a kind of primitive hunter/gatherer energy. As we collected the blueberries, partridgeberries, gooseberries and squash berries, there was a sense of preparing for winter. And indeed, as you slathered squashberry jam on your toast on a wintry January morning, adding to the enjoyment was the memory of Labour Day and picking those berries.

The other big event, marking the end of Fall was Guy Fawkes Night — a.k.a. Bonfire Night — November 5th. Not long after Halloween, it was by far the more exciting of the two. Having barely de-toxed from the sugar-glut of the Halloween pillage, on Guy Fawkes Night we dragged trees, branches, cardboard boxes from Aunt Alma's store and every other combustible thing we could gather, up to the Lookout. Nanc, Shirl and I had our bonfire together, and our parents, mostly our Dads, helped us with this. It was huge, and safely nestled on the cliff away from houses. We let her rip. Toting bags of marshmallows and long sticks we again challenged our pancreases with another load of sugar.

Our Dads carried kerosene and stuff to fuel the flames. One year my Dad and Shirl's Dad, Lloyd, played a trick on Nanc's Dad, whom I called "Uncle Lo". Having got the fire started, Lloyd and Dad encouraged Uncle Lo to throw on some kerosene. He did and lo and behold the flames died. They started all over again, repeating the same routine. By now Uncle Lo is into his rant *"Dyin', jumpin', reevin' screechin"*. Then he dropped to it. It wasn't oil he was throwing on the fire. My Dad and Lloyd had filled the can with water. They all had a big laugh, huge guffaws. Uncle Lo was a good sport, but we kids were anxious to get on with the fire. There was something wild and exciting about a big fire on a dark and cold night — and foreboding too. Because it would not be long before the snow came (if it already hadn't) and we would be hunkering down for winter.

Another tradition of late Fall was hauling up the boats. Sometimes the harbour and cove froze in the winter so boats needed to be protected. Hauling up of a boat happened just after supper. While we were eating there would be a gentle tap on the door with a request for my Dad's help on the beach at such-and-such a time to haul up whosever boat. And the same service would be offered my Father when it was time to haul up his boat.

Then when the time came the scuffle of rubber boots on the beach stones, a flurry of voices and then calm. On cue, the men would begin to sing the Jolly Poker song.

The Nipper's Harbour rendition of it was:

To me Jolly Poker
We will haul this heavy Joker.
To me Jolly Poker <u>haul</u>.

It was when they sang this last "haul" that everyone pulled in unison.

The image for me involves the rich low baritone voices of the men, the late evening darkness, and the hurried sounds of rubber boots on the beach stones, which set the stage for the dark season ahead.

Christmas was the transitioning to winter, and there's a whole story on that. But winter was more than Christmas. Snow was a vehicle for many pleasures — sledding, tobogganing, snowball fights, snow forts and snow tunnels. The possibilities were endless and the hills were just peachy for sledding. My wooden sleigh with the red runners got a good workout. But some of the fastest, most dizzying and delirious rides I ever had was on a hill next to the Government well — seldom used, and the snow with a frozen sheen of ice. Instead of using our sleds or toboggans, we would get an old piece of canvas or even cardboard, and fly down that hill, balancing on our bums, holding our knees, closing our eyes and spinning, spinning, spinning till we stopped. When we opened our eyes the bright sun would be blinding from the glare of the snow. Then there would be the long climb back up the hill to do it all over again.

It seemed that just as the events of one season were becoming a bit tiresome and monotonous, the anticipation of the transition to the next season kept the momentum going. Adjusting and accommodating to the changes became automatic. Living so close to the elements inspired a respect that allowed for an effortless relationship with Mother Nature.

Walking along the canal in Ottawa one misty Spring morning, a seagull swooped down on the walking path beside me. I chuckled to myself as I thought of us as two displaced Newfies. He gobbled up a great big juicy worm and stayed there until I walked by. I accepted it as an affirmation from the Universe. A nod from Nature, my companion from a very young age.

Visits and Visiting

V isiting was almost as natural as breathing in Nipper's Harbour — it was just a part of the ebb and flow of life. There was no technology such as telephones to formalize it — you just showed up at someone's house or someone showed up at your house. Most people were respectful of established routines and wouldn't show up for a visit on Monday morning when laundry was being done. Although if they did, they would be welcome and perhaps even offered tea amidst the racket of the old wringer washer. There was an old saying that *if you have visitors on Monday, you'll have them all the week*. Which was a bit silly because there were visitors all week anyway. Because you couldn't pick up a phone and call someone, you had to physically present yourself. This afforded an intensity of interaction, which dispensed with formalities and encouraged a raw honesty.

I honed my observational skills when visiting, and

this started at a young age. For instance, visiting my Great Aunt Pearl. There were black current bushes in her garden, which if we took the old cemetery path to her place, we would walk by on the way. The look and smell of black current bushes are as attractive as the fruit.

Going through her door, your nose met with the not unpleasant smell of Holiday tobacco. This intensified as you came closer to the kitchen, where the visit took place. Sometimes my Great Uncle Sandy (Alexander) was there, but most often it was Aunt Pearl sitting on the daybed with her hands folded, swinging the stump of her right forefinger over the thumb of her left hand. Since my Mom and I usually sat on the daybed too — either I sat on my Mom's lap or right next to her — I got a very good look at Aunt Pearl's hands. My Mom explained over and over again after these visits about why Aunt Pearl had only half her right forefinger. *Seal finger*, my Mother explained, as a result of handling raw seal meat. On one occasion that I remember we were invited to stay for an impromptu supper. Aunt Pearl served bottled seal meat (a wide range of foods could be preserved in bottles by heating and sealing) with creamed potatoes. I was haunted by the notion of Aunt Pearl's seal finger, and her serving seal meat. It all of a sudden looked very unappetizing — I concentrated on the potatoes, which was one of my favourites anyway. And appreciated the canned peaches with tinned Danish cream for dessert. That night I asked Mom to explain to me again about the seal finger.

Walt and Gladys' house was one of the first in Nipper's Harbour to have a TV. So when Mom went to visit Gladys in the harbour after supper, while they talked in the kitchen, I would sit by myself in the living room (after they turned on the generator), and watch Don Messer's Jubilee. As the Jubilee band struck up "Going to the barn dance tonight", and the square dancers in colourful matching outfits swung around the dance floor, I thought to myself this sure was an upscale version of the games we played at the church suppers. At the end of the show, Marg Osborne and Charlie Chamberlain usually belted out a church tune such as "The Old Rugged Cross". Their harmony was good, and it seemed a fitting end to the lively performance. This also was good timing for the lunch that Gladys served us before we went home. Since everyone had a lunch before they went to bed anyway, this lunch was a routine part of an evening visit. First, Gladys asked Juliet, her very spoiled dog, if she wanted to do her pee, and she would let her out in the yard. Gladys talked baby-talk to Juliet, and called herself "Nana". Sometimes she called Juliet "The Angel's Throne". Only after Juliet got nicely settled back down on the daybed, would Gladys serve lunch.

Such lunches in Nipper's Harbour consisted of

dense food: — biscuits, cheese, squares, cake, tea buns. And tea. With Carnation evaporated milk, and sugar. We climbed the 72-steps on the way home, which was one way of cancelling out some of those calories.

The two visits described were purposeful and pre-meditated. This is a mere sub-category of a much larger phenomenon. The day-to-day dropping in was more fluid and spontaneous in nature. For instance, Greta, the neighbour dropped by regularly for just a few minutes. Most often, she didn't even sit down. She stood in the entrance to our kitchen, or just inside. She would be wearing a 1950's cotton housedress; similar to the ones my Mom wore — floral and fitted at the waist. She would fold her arms across her chest and talk in serious tones to my Mother. Usually a bit of news or gossip or something of some consequence. She would leave sometimes mid-sentence because she would see her husband coming home for a meal, and she would rush to put the potatoes on to boil.

Then there was Cliff who dropped in just about every day, sometimes twice a day. He lived with a mental illness, manifesting itself in repetitive speech patterns, sudden outbursts of laughter, and rigid body movements. Nobody tried to suppress these symptoms with medications. Cliff lived his life with a great degree of freedom, and one of the things he enjoyed doing was visiting. He was welcome in many homes, including ours and was given many meals, because one of his greatest pleasures was eating. He often waltzed in unceremoniously, without taking off his boots, and as the snow melted on the kitchen floor, he would gently tap-tap his feet on the water. My Mom would run and get a mop and ask him to lift his feet while she wiped up the water. Cliff would giggle and comply, all the while saying, "I don't mind you my lovie, I don't mind you. No, no, no! Ha, ha ha!" Sometimes he would pick up the Eaton's catalogue if it were lying around, and go to the women's lingerie section. My Mom would ask him what he was looking at, and he would do one of his "Ha, ha, ha-s" while saying "I knows how far to go, my lovie. I knows how far to go. EEEEE! Ha! Ha! Ha!"

It was usually a Saturday night when Walt and Gladys would come over, if it were time for Dad to have a haircut. Walt was phenomenally multi-talented. He read and taught music, played the organ in church, cut hair, knitted and sewed, in addition to his regular job at L.J. Noble & Sons. Walt cut Dad's hair in the kitchen. Dad sat on a kitchen chair with his back to Walt. Walt held the hair clippers in one hand and scissors in the other. I'm guessing he was ambidextrous as well as everything else. Walt would chat up a storm when he was cutting hair, tut-tutting about this and that. Mom would be hovering around with a broom and dustpan, sweeping up the hair. And if Cliff dropped in with wet boots in the midst of it all, it became a lovely mess.

Effie, Mom's friend, visited our house regularly when I was very young. She had no children of her own, but loved kids. She was gentle and kind, and had a soft and soothing voice which practically lulled me to sleep as she read my favourite book aloud to me, *Little Red Riding Hood* – the one with the popup pictures. My heart invariably started to race when we got to the wolf part, but snuggled safely in Effie's armpit, I weathered this storm over and over.

The Minister was expected to visit his parishioners on schedule, especially the sick and elderly members. However, all members of the congregation were on his wider rotation. I would try not to be home when the minister came, because it was more formal than with other visitors. And it always ended with him praying, which I found kind of intimidating. It just seemed more of an adult thing. You could dodge those visits by being out and about and scouting the route that the minister might be on any given day. Despite my best efforts, there was the odd occasion when I got trapped in the house, as the minister knocked on the door.

Relatives and neighbours kept the rhythm of visiting going quite consistently although the pace varied with the seasons. In the winter, for instance, men visited more, because it was the down season for their work. Uncle Ches (not my real uncle, but he might as well have been) often came over at night for a yarn with my Dad. They talked about hunting seals, fishing and the church. Uncle Ches was passionate about everything. He had a warm, expressive face, and gesticulated with his hands to make a point. A deeply religious man, he would often break into singing if he were discussing matters of the church with my Dad. One of his favourites was:

With his loving hand to guide
Let the clouds above me roll
And the billows in their fury
Dash around me.
I can brave the wildest storm
With his glory in my soul.
I can sing amidst the tempest
Praise the Lord.

He loved hymns that had to do with the ocean and storms because it was a metaphor he lived every day.

Aunt Alma (Uncle Ches' wife) was a good friend of my Mom's. She was loving and kind like my Uncle Ches. They had no children, and were indulgent of their only niece, Norma, as well as those whom they had informally adopted.

Every Easter, Aunt Alma made and delivered homemade Easter eggs — decorated with flowers and squiggles with our names on them. They were a work of art, and a work of love.

Aunt Alma and Uncle Ches lived in the same house as Uncle Ches' parents, whom we called Uncle Hig (actually "Edgar") and Aunt Suse. They lived in a two-story house. The kitchen was large, painted a creamy yellow, and in the corner, hanging from the ceiling, was a cage holding a very spoiled blue budgie bird, "Tippy". The house was quite Ches-centric and the budgie reflected this in his vocabulary. He made statements including "Ches gone to church", "Ches gone in the harbour", "Ches is comin", and "Shut up your lip Ches". The only other thing he said not related to Ches was, "Tippy pretty bird". If you happened to drop in on Tippy's bath day, stand clear! Aunt Suse would get a pan of water and put it on the kitchen table. There would be the routine of getting the temperature just right: not too hot, not too cold, just tepid for the delicate little bird. Aunt Suse would dab and flap about in the pan of water, wiping her hands on her apron, before Aunt Alma opened the birdcage. Tippy would get all excited. He didn't like having a bath, but he enjoyed the attention. He would start repeating all the words he knew as he flew and flapped about while Aunt Suse tried to wash his feathers. By the end, it was Aunt Suse herself who had the bath, with Tippy lucky to have gotten a lick and a promise. He would go back to his cage, exhausted from the ordeal, and Aunt Suse muttering "The **bloomian** bird" as she started to clean up the mess.

When we were about 7 or 8 years old, Shirl, Nanc, and I had our own visiting circuit that had largely to do with dropping in on newly married couples that had just had a baby — ostensibly to see the baby, because we, after all, were children. But really, we went there to observe. We noted the awkwardness and lack of finesse of some of these young women, comparing them to the smoothness of our own mothers' housekeeping skills. We would watch with interest as they struggled to make a pan of Rice Krispie squares, and go home to an assortment of fresh baking. Shirl and I in particular specialized in the study of newly married couples with babies. My visiting with Nanc was more focused. She took Avon orders and delivered them for her mother. I was the accomplice. This routine gave me access to virtually every home in the outport, and I knew with some degree of accuracy the favourite fragrances and Avon items in each place. Talcum powder was popular. *Here's my Heart* and *To a Wild Rose* were the two frequent requests. Cream sachets came in ornate little jars. *Here's my Heart* in a blue jar — and *To a Wild Rose* in pink and white.

I haven't spoken about long-stay houseguests, as

that is a category of visiting quite separate from the day-to-day variety.

The coming of the road and telephones signalled the beginning of the end of this sort of visiting.

Gradually, over the years, the spontaneity receded, and visiting became more scheduled; as people became more connected to the outside, they became less connected to each other.

Undoubtedly there are those who would argue the pros and cons of this change. In my romanticized version of the whole experience I would not have exchanged that aspect of life for anything. Visiting was almost as important as play.

Health Care

My Great Grandmother, as I have said before, lived into her 90s, and did not suffer from any major disease. But she did have a bit of arthritis, or rheumatism as she referred to it. "Me rheumatic, you" was actually what she said. She didn't pay a lot of heed to it, but it did slow her movements, so once per week she took one Templeton's TRC capsule. This is how it went. First, she poured a cup of tea into a china cup on a saucer. Then she removed the saucer and separated the capsule, pouring the granules into her saucer. She disposed of the casing, by throwing it into the stove. I suspect she didn't believe in swallowing plastic. Then she poured some of her tea on top of the grains of the TRC capsule in her saucer and gently swished it around. She drank it slowly from the saucer until it was all gone. And put the cup back on the saucer where it belonged. As far as I know this is the only medical procedure my great Grandmother ever had.

Well, she gave birth to her three children: my Grandma, Great Uncle Will and Great Uncle Fred, but that was eons ago. Because Great Grandmother was a positive and calm person, I suspect the births were calm and uneventful with the assistance of a midwife at home. One lovely sunny summer day she died. She was sitting outside on the front porch — laughing and talking one minute — to die the next.

Historically, there had been an English doctor stationed in Nipper's Harbour. I recall some of the older people referring to "Dr. Coulter", and Walt's house had been the original clinic/dispensary, as well as living space for the doctor and his family. Over time Walt had clearly changed the medical area to a living space, but I do recall it was a big house, as I used to visit there when my Mom went to have a yarn with Walt's wife Gladys.

There were three options for the residents of Nipper's Harbour to see a doctor in the days before the road was built. They weren't easy options, but the only ones available to us. Tilt Cove, a 2-hour boat ride away, was a mining town, and they had a Dr. Gillespie and a nurse (Mrs. Gillespie), which comprised a clinic. I believe they also dispensed medication. Mrs. Gillespie came to Nipper's Harbour to give us kids our inoculations. This was done either at school or in Aunt Alma's front-porch-cum-clinic.

Going to Tilt Cove, going anywhere, even for medical reasons, was an adventure. While we were there, we ate our mid-day meal in the Miners' Mess Hall, the closest thing to a restaurant within a wide radius of Nipper's Harbour. It was a cafeteria-style arrangement, and the memories of it are fleeting. I remember more clearly a store, perhaps a drugstore, and an arrangement of candy different from what I was used to. Raspberry drops — hard candy with a bumpy surface representing raspberry seeds, in a see-through bag hanging on a display hook. Visually very appealing.

The major medical place was the Notre Dame Bay Memorial Hospital in Twillingate. Too far to go by motorboat, but accessible by steamer. So you could go by one of the steamers, the S.S. Hopedale or the S.S. Springdale, to Twillingate, and Dr. Olds. The steamers landed at the Government Wharf on the South side of the harbour. You needed a taxi to get to the North side where the hospital was located. The hospital was on a hill and beneath that hill was a boarding house, owned and operated by the Stockley family. This is where we stayed. You had to stay there until the next available steamer. There was no exact way of knowing when the next steamer would swing by on its way to your part of the coast. So if the steamer's whistle blew in the middle of the night, you quickly pulled yourself together to get in the cab to the wharf. Fortunately, Mr. Stockley was also the taxi driver.

This experience of steamers, cars, hospital, doctors, taxi drivers and a boarding house was a dizzying experience for me as a child. It was like going to New York City, I supposed – very exciting and stimulating.

Perhaps not so exciting was the occasion my Mom was taken away on the steamer in the middle of the night. I was barely five years old. I was awakened by somebody and taken to the kitchen. Prostrate on the daybed was my Mom. People were hovering around her, including my Aunt Alma. My Mom was pale and uncommunicative. I knelt on a kitchen chair hugging the back, not understanding what was going on. People were coming and going out the door, and all of a sudden I was sent over to kiss my Mom on the cheek. She did not respond. They took her away on a stretcher out the door. My Great Aunt Hagar took me to bed, covered me up, tucked me in, gently brushed my forehead and kissed me. What I now know is my Mother was taken to Twillingate Hospital on a steamer that called into port to get her after a flurry of telegrams. What I also know is that many of the people tending to her that night thought she was going to die, and although I had no frame of reference for this, I was just aware of overwhelming sadness and loss. There were no telephones to keep us abreast of her condition.

My Aunt Jean was enlisted to stay with me during

my Mother's absence. My Dad and other relatives were also around. On Saturday, as custom dictated, we had pea soup for lunch. I remember the stone-colour soup bowl with the wide rim, and the pea soup with the large pieces of carrot floating around in it. I took the soup-spoon and stirred and stirred. I looked up and my Aunt Jean with her enormous blue eyes and flaming red hair said in her lilting voice, "What's the matter, my little dear — don't like the soup?" "Mom", I said, "only puts half a carrot in hers". She stifled the giggle but it became a long-standing family joke.

My Mom came home two weeks later. Two weeks to a five-year old is a very long time. For months she lay down immediately after she ate, so the food would go into her stomach. So for the meals when my Dad was away, I still felt lonely. Because I would still be dawd-ling away at my food while my Mom rested. Gradually, her 5 ft. 10 in., 117 lb. frame began to fill out, and slowly she came back.

What you don't understand as a child, you dismiss. But somehow I started to connect Twillingate Hospital and the infamous Dr. Olds with having made my Mom better and bringing her back.

When it came my turn for serious intervention at Twillingate Hospital, I already had a hopeful predis-position. The accident happened when I was nine years old. Some kid had one of those incredibly long toboggans and a dozen of us kids piled on and went ripping down a hill. The speed got out of control and we went crashing into a tree. Other than seeing a few stars and kids bodies going in all directions, all seemed fine. The next day there was blood in the toilet bowl. I showed my Mom. I was sat down and given the *birds and bees* lecture, although she was incredulous because I was only 9. So I always was a bit advanced, being able to write before I went to school and all. Then, after all that palaver of a toboggan crash and what at first appeared to be the beginning of menstruation, it turned out to be rectal bleeding. The first option for health care in Nipper's Harbour was the clinic at Tilt Cove, the second was Twillingate Hospital and so to Twillingate we went. It was all fine — great steamer ride, the taxi, Stockley's boarding house and the whole deal. Until... it was time to see the doctor. They did an enema and they didn't tell me what they were doing. I was mortified. But at least my Mom was in the room.

The third option was Springdale Hospital usually accessed by a motorboat ride to Harry's Harbour, and from there a taxi ride of about an hour to Springdale. It was a smaller hospital and not considered to have the expertise of the Twillingate facility. People went there mostly to have babies. My younger cousins all seem to have been born there. There was an English doctor — Dr. Evans, who was there a very long time.

But for several months of the year, the three medical options were not available because the harbour was packed solid with ice. Therefore there was reliance on the wisdom of traditional and natural practices, as well as the unofficial apothecary at L.J. Noble & Sons.

My first experience with natural medicine was treatment for fever when I had measles. Confined to bed, and feeling downright miserable, my Mother's announcement that she had a special medicine for me gave me some hope. Having consulted *Aunt Maggie* (not my aunt, but known to all as such, given her advanced age and wisdom), my Mom had steeped elderberry bloom. It was the most bitter, vilest thing I had ever tasted, with a foul odour, and I remember telling my Mother angrily that I thought Aunt Maggie had scraped the contents of that brew from between her toes! However, the fever subsided, whether from the brew or of its own accord is anybody's guess.

Another "natural" remedy was balsam, usually mixed with molasses. My Father was particularly partial to this remedy when he had a cold. Like me, he had a sweet tooth, and I think the molasses had a lot of appeal.

Soft bread poultices were often used for skin infections, or even for splinters. It was simply bread soaked in water and applied to the wound, which was then secured in place with gauze and tape, the latter referred to as *sticking plaster*.

Charms were used for nasty, pesky things that wouldn't go away. 'Move over, Salem'— we had powers of witchcraft in Nipper's Harbour. There was at least one woman if not more, who could make charms to be worn around the neck for a number of days, which would make boils or skin eruptions, disappear, for instance. And it worked. My Mother tells me she examined a charm my Dad wore once and found it was simply a whole nutmeg sewn into a piece of cloth. I would be interested to know if there were rituals associated with making this charm. Sufficient to say, the charms were more effective than many modern remedies for such ailments.

My Mother tells me that in Beaumont on Long Island, Newfoundland, where she grew up, there was a belief that the seventh son born into a family had special healing powers. This is an interesting fact in itself, since healing energy has been traditionally associated with women. My Mom says it was believed these seventh sons could stop bleeding, for instance, and make a toothache disappear. It was also believed that if an earthworm were placed into the hand of such a person, the worm would die. Most families in Nipper's Harbour had fewer than seven children, so this theory had no subjects to be tested. And the couple of families who had seven or more children had both genders, so a seventh son would have been rare indeed.

In medical crises or emergencies, there was no emergency room to go to. My own experience with a medical crisis occurred when I was quite young. My Mom had given me a set of broken beads to play with. I decided I would make ear-rings out of them, except there was nothing to attach these beads to my ears, so I put one in my ear, and in an effort to get it to stay put, I poked it in too far. Then I panicked, and before I knew it, had been whipped across the road to my Aunt Alma's (actually she was my Mom's cousin, but I always called her aunt). She quite calmly and serenely removed the bead with the assistance of a crochet hook. Then I was admonished never to put anything in my ear, how dangerous it was and all. But all I felt was undeniable relief.

The medicine section of L. J. Noble & Sons covered most of the medical needs in Nipper's Harbour — everything from Andrew's Liver Salts for indigestion to Dr. Chase's Nerve Food for, as the name suggests, the nerves. Essentially, all bases were covered with either what was in your own or someone else's medicine cabinet, or a trip to the informal apothecary at Noble's.

Colds, coughs and fever being a part of winter, most households would have on hand a supply of Buckley's Mixture, balsam and molasses, Antiphlogistine and Spirits of Nitre. Spirits of Nitre was a clear fluid in a small Gerald S. Doyle medicine bottle. It was almost as vile as Aunt Maggie's elderberry bloom. And hauled out the minute you spiked a fever. Never mind that it was mixed with hot water and sugar. Chest colds warranted the application of Antiphlogistine to the chest, and covered in flannel. We called it "Anti-flo" like a kindly relative. Perhaps this is why, as kids, we didn't object to it — having such a user-friendly term. Vicks VapoRub was also available and used, as were Vicks Cough Drops.

Every winter I was saddled with asthma, which in retrospect I now see linked to the coal-burning stove at home and at school. At Noble's you could purchase Rhasma tablets for asthma. These I took, along with the special prescription liquids from Dr. Gillespie in Tilt Cove. One bottle contained red liquid, the other a yellow syrup. The wheezing was disconcerting. I spent many nights propped up with pillows because I could not breathe.

Why my Mother gave me Scott's Emulsion is anybody's guess. Thick white liquid in a bottle with navy blue and orange labelling, it was referred to as a "tonic" and given for poor appetite. (Perhaps my Mother's own difficulty with eating made her over-conscientious where I was concerned.) I have never lost my appetite, but am sceptical as to the long-lasting effects of Scott's Emulsion.

Being a child, I had little or no need for products for the gastro-intestinal track, but adults had any number of remedies for an upset stomach. These included two Gerald S. Doyle remedies, Essence of Peppermint and Essence of Ginger Wine, as well as Milk of Magnesia, Radways Ready Relief, and rum or brandy mixed with sugar and water.

On one occasion, Mr. Sacrey came into our house complaining of "a bad stomach", and asking my Mother if she had any Radways. My Mom offered to mix a cup with a portion of the medicine and some boiling water, to which he responded with a request for the bottle as it was. He removed his glasses and placed them on the kitchen table. He removed his dentures and placed them besides his glasses. He unscrewed the stopper from the Radways container, tipped the bottle to his sunken lips, and drank lustily. My Mom's dark eyes sat on her cheeks in astonishment. One can only imagine what this stuff was to the digestive track: what Drain-o is to the pipes.

Constipation was a concern given the lack of fresh fruit and fresh vegetables in the diet, and in general, lack of fibre. Carter's Little Liver Pills, Castor Oil, X-Lax, and Tru-Lax were available to deal with this ailment.

Other old-people ailments included:

-   Headaches: instead of reaching immediately for an aspirin, although they were available, people were more likely to try "vinegar paper". Quite simply this was a piece of sturdy brown wrapping paper soaked in vinegar and placed on the forehead.

-   Templeton's TRCs is what old people took for arthritis, but if my Great Grandmother was any example, there would not have been a great demand because she used them sparingly.

-   Kidney ailments were addressed with Dodd's Kidney Pills. They came in a little round box, and sat neatly in the medicine cabinet.

-   Also in the medicine cabinet were Mercurochrome and iodine, both dispensed in eyedropper form, and used on cuts and wounds. Fishermen had lots of cuts, blisters, boils and wounds. Handling hooks, knives, rough ropes, navigating cold salt water, and climbing rocks came with a risk of skin abrasions. "Dragon's Blood" purchased at Noble's was curious stuff. A thick dark red paste was cut and melted with a hot knife, and applied to the wound. Upon removal a few days later the wound would typically be completely healed. This product must have come from England.

Other than too much salt in their diet (of necessity, because of lack of refrigeration), people lived quite healthy lives. They worked hard, walked everywhere, and ate wholesome food, with little or no processed food. So the medicines at Noble's were quite sufficient.

I'm not convinced modern medicine has brought us much further ahead. I keep a bottle of ginger wine in our pantry cupboard. If I feel a little squeamish or feel a cold coming on, sometimes I mix a drop with some sugar in a cup of boiling water. I would think it brings more comfort to my soul than it does to my body.

The Post Office

I t was a small dark-green building on the footpath that meandered through the harbour on the way to L.J. Noble & Sons and the Government Wharf. This building, though humble in appearance, held great respect from me when I was a kid. Really, it was the centre of operations on all kinds of levels, both formal and informal. I was there, at least a couple of times a week, reflecting the frequency of the mail delivery. And if there was stuff to be mailed or stamps to be bought, sometimes I was there more often.

I thought Gord Windsor the postmaster was without question the smartest creature on Earth. Not only could this guy sort mail, do money orders, collect for C.O.D packages and all that, but he also sent and received telegrams. Morse code was my introduction to tele-communications. Gord doing the dot-dash routine, with a cigarette dangling from his lips, his eyes all squinted up, either typing the message as it was coming through or executing the dot-dash combinations himself. Good news, bad news, he was the first to know. Bad news was placed in a pink envelope, and Gord shut down the office while he walked to the person's home to hand-deliver it. People got nervous if they saw Gord arriving with a pink envelope and they got curious if they saw him going to someone else's home with the dreaded pink message.

The mail arrived by boat in the summer, and dog-team in the winter. Without question the summer schedule was more reliable and predictable. Winter was tricky, with snowstorms and all.

The big mail days were the arrival of Eaton's and Simpson's catalogues, and the days leading up to Christmas with the arrival of hundreds of Christmas cards. Here's how it went. You stood in the small office, separated from Gord by the open wicket, and a closed door. Gord pulled the mail by handfuls from the bag and started calling out the names of people on the envelopes. If someone was there to take it, his or her hand flew up to the wicket to receive it. Pre-Christmas was tricky because the office would be jammed with people. Sometimes I thought I would smother, either suffocated by the wet wool coats of the adults standing in front of me, or the cigarette smoke of the smokers all around me. But you persevered, and by the time you sputtered out of there, gasping for air, you were sure that the discomfort was all worth it. A letter from your cousin, a bunch of Christmas cards, the Eaton's catalogue, made it all worthwhile.

Other times at the Office were more tranquil. There were the lazy summer days I strolled over there with my Mom, perhaps just to mail a letter or buy stamps. There might be another adult that she casually chatted with, while I cased out what was happening — Gord sending a message, or sometimes the graffiti on the window-sill. Initials, hearts, and the outline of a person done in nail punctures. It made me want to connect the dots and colour it in, like I did in my colouring book.

Some trips to the Office were more intense. Such as when Nancy had to buy a money order for an Avon shipment. Her Mother was the Avon representative for Nipper's Harbour. Well, officially. But Nancy at the grand old age of nine or ten years old was doing the high finance. With money orders you had to fill out a form, not unlike writing a cheque, with carbon copies for yourself and the post office. I used to feel like a Brinks driver bringing up the rear. We took the responsibility quite seriously. Sometimes adults laughed at us because we were a bit like little old ladies — Nancy, Shirley and I. But the sense of responsibility paid off in many ways. We each became quite successful in our own fields in life, and not surprisingly ended up in careers that carried quite a lot of responsibility.

The Post Office was our only connection with the outside world. There were no phones, no cars, no road. To be specific, Gord was our only immediate connection with the outside world because he was the only wireless operator. Letters were very important.

Two of my Mom's sisters lived in Toronto. Letters from them were like gold. I remember the photographs of cousins I had never seen, and my Mom's stories of her sisters when they were growing up. It all sounded very remote and exotic. I remember the Toronto postmark on those letters, trying to imagine what it was like there, noting the background in the enclosed photographs. Roads! Paved streets, cars — quite a concept.

That small dark green clapboard Post Office is forever etched in my memory. It represented greater possibilities, hopes, dreams, the intangible becoming tangible, and the interconnectedness of us all. Twice a week I was reminded that there was something more than Nipper's Harbour. And now I go back in my mind to Nipper's Harbour, and sometimes the Post office, and know that this is what keeps me grounded.

L.J. Noble & Sons

*I*t wasn't like the typical General Store one might imagine or as depicted in a small-town TV show. Because it was more than a general store, and it wasn't the only store in Nipper's Harbour. There was the Union Store, a variation on the theme of L.J. Noble & Sons (referred to by the locals as "Noble's"), two small stores in the cove, "Alma's" and "Sterling's", and a "Restaurant" in the bottom of the harbour referred to as "Les'". Actually the latter wasn't a restaurant as one would think, but a hangout for young people to smoke, play cards and drink coca-cola from those bottles shaped like a female body. They sold an assortment of confectionary items, cigarettes, and the odd bits of packaged food. The overview of all the stores is merely to provide context.

There were two ways to get to Noble's — boat and "shank's pony", i.e. walking. Usually we walked. Up three sets of steps from the cove, down 72 steps to the harbour and through the harbour, down a few more steps to the store, which was located adjacent to the Government Wharf, where the steamers docked. Noble's also had its own wharf connected with the store, and if we got a ride to the store in a motor boat, then we landed at that wharf and climbed up the steps to the landing. Then there were two ways to get into the actual store. One was to walk through to a set of stairs accessed from the outside. The other was to walk into the massive storage area, and up some stairs that let you in to the back of the store near the "office". If you took the latter option, there was a strong odour of rope and **oakum** and salt and other smells related to the salt-fish industry. If you had to package this smell you might call it "*Eau de Salt Fish*".

If there had been an elevator shaft in Noble's, it would have had 4 stops, maybe 5, because I think there might have been another storage area below the wharf landing area, where they stored salt. But I wasn't too interested in salt as a kid. Anyhow, on the main level they displayed groceries, some dishes, toiletries such as soap and toothpaste, a small cosmetics section with Noxzema skin cream, nail polish, and Evening in Paris cologne; a pharmaceuticals section with products from Gerald S. Doyle, such as Spirits of Nitre, Essence of Peppermint, and Ginger Wine. Other medicines sold from this area of the store were Cod Liver Oil, Castor

Oil, Epsom salts, Scott's Emulsion, Templeton's TRCs, Carter's Little Liver Pills and Dodd's Kidney Pills. There was an ointment called "Dragon's Blood" which fishermen applied to open sores or wounds; this product I suspect might have come from England. I really have seen nothing like it since that time. They also supplied the products for dressing a wound such as sterilized gauze and tape.

At the back near the office was stuff related to fishing, such as rubber boots, sou'westers, **oil clothes**, and things like nails, screws, light bulbs. And there were cooking pots too, down in that section.

Up the stairs from the main level was the dry goods section. Clothing, linens, yarn, greeting cards, gift-wrap, socks, nylons, and shoes. There was also a seasonal section that featured children's toys, although these might also be displayed in an area on the main floor, depending on space availability. Christmas displays weren't the only seasonal items. Wreaths and sprays made of artificial flowers and greenery were displayed usually at the back of the store when somebody died. Indeed, one could go into Noble's, and meet somebody buying a wreath or a spray without any previous knowledge that someone had died. This could put one in a real pickle, especially if it was a wreath that was being purchased. A wreath — larger and more expensive, usually was bought for a relative or good friend.

Sprays—smaller and less expensive were purchased as a sign of acknowledgement and respect, but indicated greater emotional distance. So, it would be safe to say, "Who died, you?" to someone buying a spray. But you might wait and ask the clerk that question after the person buying a big wreath had left the store.

And above the dry goods section was another level, which was essentially dry goods storage. This was not open to the public, but I was allowed in there a couple of times with my Mom and her friend Effie who worked in the store. Actually Effie was the wife of the manager. So this peek into the secret world of Noble's was thrilling beyond words.

The level shared with the wharf landing had literally tons of stuff in storage. Everything they sold in the store and then some. Because the fishing supplies such as twine, fishing net material, rope, salt, **oakum**, engine oil, engine parts, were stored in the bowels of the store or in one of their other buildings on the premises. This is not what I was interested in as a child.

It was the glass case at the front that had the chocolate bars, and the jars that had the English toffee, Purity peppermint knobs, and Purity common candy that drew me like a magnet. The chocolate was mostly from England — Needlers' solid chocolate bars, but in an assortment of flavours, including orange, coffee, strawberry and pineapple. Lowney, Cadbury and Nestle products were also sold, but it's Needlers that stands out in my mind, because they were my favourite and can no longer be found. Dulac potato chips in red and silver bags were also delicious. Shirley Andrews, one of the clerks, kept a bottle of tomato Ketchup under the counter, and when Nancy, Shirley and I bought chips, she would surreptitiously haul this contraband from under the counter and give us a little dab inside the bag in which we dipped each crunchy morsel. Candy was counted out into little paper bags and then twisted at the top. We would twist and untwist these bags for each candy eaten. By the time the candy was finished, the bag was rather ratty.

Most supplies were on shelves behind the counter. As you asked for each item, the clerk went to the shelf and brought it to the counter. It was labour intensive, because then each item was hand written onto a counter bill. When you had finished, the counter bill was totalled, the products wrapped carefully into brown paper taken from a huge roll, where it was pulled and torn off along the serrated edge. String from a large spool secured the package. Some of the clerks knew a trick for breaking the string without having to use scissors. I thought that was quite clever, and wondered if when I grew up I would get a job in the store and handle the packaging as cleverly as Shirley Andrews and my Great Aunt Nellie, one of the other clerks in the store. Aunt Nellie was quite slick in the numbers department — adding up counter bills at lightning speed, snapping the string without the use of scissors. All the while sporting three rollers in the front of her hair, while the rest of it was tied in a scarf — and knotted behind the rollers in an almost perfect replica of Mrs. Sharples from Coronation Street.

On the counter, in addition to wrapping paper, string, counter bill books and writing pens, were domes. Underneath one dome was a humungous round of rat-trap cheese. Under the other couple of domes were slab bacon, ham and bologna. Also machete-type knives to cut off pieces of those products, that were duly plopped onto waxed paper and weighed on the scales. Then the waxed paper was wrapped into a small segment of brown paper, and rewrapped into the lager parcels. There were no grocery bags — a foreign concept. There were, however, small bags for just small items, mostly for candy.

Because my Father, as most fishermen in Nipper's Harbour, sold their fish to Noble's (as well as the Union Store) we had a running account with them. This harkens back to the days of the barter system. So, every Fall, the bills were collected and offset against what had been shipped. The balance was paid in cash.

Not just the fishermen in Nipper's Harbour shipped to the businesses in Nipper's Harbour. Boats from outside the community were routinely tied up to the wharf.

Boats from Smith's Harbour, Rogue's Harbour, Middle Arm, Burlington, Indian Burying Place, Snook's Arm and Round Harbour were frequent visitors, and if one of the outsiders was at the counter, you could hang around the store a very long time waiting for service. Because they sold in bulk — Noble's became like Costco when customers from visiting boats were doing business. Unlike us, they couldn't go to the store every day.

At the back of the store were benches where you could sit. Only men did this.[‡] The back of Noble's had an intensity of conversation amongst the men . Some of them smoked pipes, and there was great animation as they conferred about fishing, sealing, the government, Joey Smallwood, trap berths, costal boats, death, the new minister, and what it was like during "the war" (WW II) and rations. The smell of Holiday pipe tobacco, the cadence of baritone voices, the laughter, the poignant pauses in conversation as great pronouncements were pondered, provided a backdrop to what was going on at the counter. For us kids, men's chatter was simply 'white noise'.

It would have been improper for women to hang out at the back of the store. They stood at the counters and negotiated groceries or went upstairs to the dry

---

[‡] *I used to be reminded of this when I lived in the Danforth District in Toronto and saw the coffee houses with all the old Greek fellows hanging out drinking espresso.*

goods to buy socks and underwear or greeting cards. They chatted with other women but in a more incidental way than the men at the back who were having big yarns. They talked about children, elders, sickness, health, food, visitors, laundry and the weather.

As kids, for the most part, we did not talk in the store. We spent our allowance, got our dab of Ketchup from Shirley Andrews, and observed everything that was going on. And there was lots going on. We would talk about it on the walk home. What one of us didn't observe, the other one did.

Noble's was a truly eclectic experience — a centre of trade, business and recreation all rolled into one. The Orange Crush sign on Noble's store, the smell of cod, the sound of motorboats, and the taste of lukewarm root beer or cream soda are lovely memories.

School Days

My education began before I started school. There were two sources — the older kids I played with, who, when we played school, had me as the student, because they knew more than I did. And my Uncle Cyril who taught me to write. But this early exposure to book learning did not make the transition to being a formal student any easier.

I resisted going to school. That first day I was all dressed up in new clothes, including a maroon blazer with piping around the edge, matching beret, and a book-bag that went over my shoulder, with an apple for recess in the front pouch. I got halfway down the garden, and announced to my Mother that I was not going to school. When she tried to use some moral authority to convince me otherwise, I countered with the accusation that she was just sending me to school to get rid of me. She burst into tears.

The next day my Father carried me to school in his arms, me kicking, flailing and being altogether hysterical. He opened the door and set me down and left. Awakening from my blinding rage, I became aware of the quietness in the room — the teacher and all the kids staring at me. Wiping tears and mucus on the sleeve of my new blazer I allowed myself to be escorted to my desk. I was embarrassed.

After that I loved school. Never missed a day, begged to go when I was sick, and performed above expectations.

School for me was a two-room clapboard building adjacent to the United Church. It was the United Church School. There was a one-room Anglican School in the harbour. Not bad for a community of 350 people. So Kindergarten to Grade six was in one room and Grades seven to eleven in the other room. There was an upstairs accessed by stairs from the outside, but this facility was used by the church congregation for social functions and sometimes meetings or mid-week services such as Lenten services.

Each classroom had a coal- and wood-burning stove, a large chalkboard behind the teacher's large wooden desk, wooden desks and chairs for the kids, a globe, maps on the walls and a very large coronation picture of the Queen. There was a room about the size of a broom-closet that was the "library" — a small collection of books, which I sometimes poked around in after my seat-work was finished.

It could get very cold in the winter, so cold that occasionally the teacher let us sit on long wooden benches near the stove to do our work. We would dramatize how cold it was by keeping on our mittens, perhaps in the faint hope that the teacher would let us go home early. This rarely happened, but never dampen-ed our hopes of a miracle, nor our efforts to convince our teacher just how cold we were.

Every year we had a new teacher. September was great — new books, new teacher, new exercise books and pens and erasers. Even the weather was nice in Newfoundland in September, usually. Sunny, cool, clear and clean.

Every morning I went across the road to Nancy's house to wait for her to walk to school. She was older than I — two grades ahead, which she felt gave her the right to dictate the shots, so I just had to wait. Nanc was not a morning person; her body movements were methodical at the beginning of the day. I would be sitting on the daybed in the kitchen with my coat on, while Nanc noshed languidly on her toasted raspberry jam and bacon sandwich. There would be intermittent prompts from her mother to "hurry up", while I sweated from the heat of my outer clothes, as well as from the anxiety of getting to school on time. The radio was tuned into "Reverend Matthews". We were usually tearing out the door as the day's episode of Reverend Matthews was ending. And it always ended on a dramatic note — a car crash (for which we had no frame of reference, but the tension was enhanced by sound effects and music), or bad news or other bait to get you to tune in the next day.

By the time we got to school, I was a bag of nerves! Nanc and I would be crash landing at our desks as the bell rang. It was a relief and respite to be at school.

Each morning after the bell was rung, and before we started our schoolwork, we had prayers. We had navy blue United Church prayer books, a different prayer for each day of the week, followed by the Lord's Prayer. We knew these prayers by heart I suspect, but each day we trotted out the blue books and read the prayers, because that's just what you did.

In a classroom with six grades, there's not a lot of individual attention. But great entertainment. In the lower grades, you get to find out what's happening in the higher grades, and can tune into and learn anything that is being taught. You learn how to absorb this on your own and set your own objectives and structure. Transition to University was a cakewalk for me, and I attribute this to how I learned *how* to learn in that two-room school in Nipper's Harbour.

The teachers were an interesting lot. Grade two was Miss Francis, who wore pointed bras (French bras I think they were called). As she leaned over my desk and I got a close-up view of her chest I became increasingly alarmed that as I grew up this would happen to me. I would have pointy appendages growing out of my chest. Every night I checked myself out, fretting about the possibility of this process starting any time soon.

Mr. Gillingham taught grade three. I categorized him in my mind as a boy teacher. He wore after-shave lotion. That's what I remember — the ever-present fragrance, which became more pronounced when he walked by your desk — after-shave lotion mixed with the smell of chalk residue on his hands.

Miss West, in Grade four, was an unusual sort. She had a nervous habit of chewing the back of her hand when she was concentrating or focusing on something. For example, before she wrote on the chalkboard, she would hold a piece of chalk and nosh on the back of her hand as she consulted the book on her desk. I couldn't make sense of this behaviour, as I had never observed it before then. When I got home, I would sometimes nosh the back of my hand, just to see what it felt like, or if anything spectacular would happen, like a burst of learning or great insight. In Grade four we were introduced to geography — a green book whose first chapter focused on Africa and a boy named Bunga, a Pygmy who lived in the jungle.

Grade five was a wonderful year. Our teacher, Miss

Upward, was a good teacher and really pretty. She had long, thick, wavy hair and a happy smile. Newfoundland history was part of the curriculum that year, and I felt I was quite grown up.

Grade six brought us Miss Locke. The first day of school she wore a white dress, a green bangle bracelet, and sported frosty pink nail polish. I knew straight away that we had landed a fashion plate, and I was going to have my hands full keeping tabs on her wardrobe. Which I did, all year. On my report card, she wrote that my parents should encourage me to read all I could. I took that to heart and that summer spent most of the time sitting on the couch in our front porch reading novels. Curious, I thought, how she could have known about how I loved to read. But to have it confirmed like this was quite wonderful.

Grade seven was the big transition year to the classroom with the higher grades with my next boy teacher, Mr. Button. Canadian history that year, which I found really boring and quite disconnected with. I just memorized the text for my tests and exams, but felt it had nothing to do with my frame of reference.

Grade eight was an even greater transition year — on all levels. That was the year the road came through to Nipper's Harbour, and it was my last year in that school. Mrs. Florence was my teacher, and she taught her own son, Jim, who was in Grade eleven — the last year before university. She spent quite a lot of her time focused on the Grade eleven curriculum. Macbeth was quite familiar to me when I got to it three years later. I was studying British history that year in grade eight, which to me had much greater relevance, and was reinforced by Mrs. Florence, a Monarchist of the first order.

There was no plumbing in the school. At recess time, water could be accessed from a running brook just steps from the door of the classroom of the lower grades. There was an outhouse across the road, perched precariously over a cliff. Generally this was used only in dire emergencies. Washroom breaks were taken when you went home for lunch.

In 1966 it all changed. As they blasted through the cliffs and built the road, the footpaths and steps disappeared. Life would never be the same again, including school. In Grade nine I went away to school and came home on weekends. And in Grades ten and eleven we went by bus to High School. But that's another story.

School in Nipper's Harbour is what prepared me for life, where I learned to learn, and be responsible for my own learning. It was a great part of my educational journey, and a solid foundation for everything up to and including graduate school at the University of Toronto.

Root Cellars
and the Government Well

Roaring around Sweden a few years ago, we visited a pioneer village. A major feature was the thatched roofs of the houses. I was immediately triggered back to our old root cellar in Nipper's Harbour.

J ust outside our fence at the back door, across a narrow footpath was our root cellar. The one that belonged to our family. This is in contrast to the short walk to the Government Well, which belonged to the community.

The cellar was an aboveground structure, packed inside with sods. Grass and weeds grew on the roof, which made it an attractive "drive-thru" for the many sheep that roamed freely all over the cove.

The door to the cellar was opened and closed by a

long slab of wood. I didn't like going into the cellar. It was dark. My mother always took a flashlight when she went out there to fetch stuff. It was cool and damp and mouldy – dreary and unpleasant. And bugs to boot. Creepy crawlies and spiders that luxuriated in that dark damp atmosphere. There were super-deluxe spider webs to greet you as you opened that door.

The cellar's capacity was large, although I never actually went all the way in because that would have totally freaked me out. The amount of supplies stored in there was vast. Root vegetables were bought in the Fall from farmers in Rattling Brook and King's Point (more pastoral locations than rugged, rocky Nipper's Harbour). Barrels of potatoes, turnips, carrots, cabbage, beets and parsnips were purchased and stored. At Christmas time a box of Red Delicious apples; each apple individually wrapped in paper with blue lettering was stored there.

Shelves in the cellar had mason jars full of everything imaginable: pickles and jams, blueberries and raspberries in syrup, salmon, rabbits, turrs (a local species of seabirds, also called murres) and seal meat.

The temperature in the cellar preserved its contents for a long time. Cool, to keep things from freezing in the winter and from spoiling in summer.

There was quite a lot of grass and weeds around and on top of the root cellar. Stinging nettles (known locally as "stingers") grew prolifically, which also contributed to my reticence about going out there.

The cellar was such an integral part of the natural landscape, it didn't really look like anything man-made. It blended with the rugged mounds and turf, stingers and all. If you walked past it in a hurry, and didn't know it was there you might have mistaken it for an old burial ground, or outgrowth of some sort. The more I think about that old root cellar, the more respect I have for it. I wish now I had screwed up the courage at least once, to have grabbed the flashlight and gone in and had a good look around.

If you followed the old footpath from our cellar, it would take you across a grassy meadow and up a slight incline to the Government Well. The sheep used that path quite a bit too, so you had to watch where you walked because there was a lot of sheep poop to be dodged. In the summer the flies would be quite attracted to the sheep manure — great big blue flies, the size of small helicopters would be in a frenzy. So walking up to the Well was a bit of an obstacle course — navigating the sheep's droppings, the monster flies and the stingers.

On the outside the Well could have been mistaken for an outhouse. Same architecture, identical structure. On the inside, the hole was definitely bigger than an outhouse. Although we had running water as far back as I can remember, I do also remember that others didn't, and can recall people going to and from the well with water buckets. But even those who had running water used the well for another purpose in the summer. This was to cool Jell-O. Having made the Jell-O and enclosed it in a jar with a tight-fitting lid, a string was fastened around the lid and it was lowered into the well and left there until it was time to have it for dessert. Magically, the warm runny liquid solidified in the coldness of that water. Often for Sunday supper it was combined with tinned fruit and tinned Danish cream for dessert .

The well and the cellar were symbols of life, for they provided what was necessary to survive in an isolated and rugged place. Their profound simplicity parallels, for me, the power of the Eucharistic Meal. For without them, life would not have been possible.

Church

*I*t was on a hill, a pinnacle really, between the cove where we lived, and the harbour: the United Church, and it was next door to the United Church School.

As it was originally a Methodist Church (before they and the Presbyterians — well, some of them — and the Congregationalists joined forces), its design and structure were identical to other Methodist Churches. Wide steps going up to the front entrance, a steeple on the left and a dome on the right, which was the bell tower. Inside there was a wide mid-section flanked on either side by an aisle, and on either side of the aisle was a seating section. At the front, framing the altar and pulpit were seats that ran perpendicular to the main pews. In my memory these sections were used for Sunday School classes. I distinctly remember my primary class being in the section on the left, and being taught the basics by a kindly, gentle woman, Sabina, who told us God loved us and that we (Nanc, Shirl and I) were nice little girls. After our classes, we sat back in the mid-section, and sang a hymn before we went home. Shirl routinely rocked back and forth when she sang. Subtle, but she really rocked to the beat of "Jesus loves me", and "Jesus bids us shine". And because I always sat beside her and did whatever she did, I rocked too. Couldn't help it.

The choir loft was in two sections and was located above the pulpit. There was a set of stairs to each side of the choir loft from the main sanctuary. The two sides of the choir loft were gender-specific. On the left were the females and on the right the males. In the middle was the organ, with the organist facing the choir, and his back to the sanctuary. But there was an elaborate system of lights and mirrors on the organ, so that the organist could see clearly to the back of the church. This facilitated his being able to time the music and take an appropriate break when the ushers came forward with the offering from the back of the church.

Our chief organist was Walt. He moved his body a lot when he played the organ, and the topknot on the top of his head swung around like an aerial. He also counted the beats to the bar as he played. I know this because I was in the Junior Choir from the age of six years, and observed everything from that choir loft. Walt's soft rhythmic counting used to sort of throw me off, and I'd want to say numbers instead of the words to the hymn. Between Walt's counting and Shirl's rocking and my propensity to imitate, it's a wonder I didn't become a professional dancer. But alas, dancing was frowned upon in the United Church, it being still connected to its Methodist roots.

Before joining Junior Choir, I still attended church. But because my parents sat close to the front in the mid-section, and because you're not allowed to turn around, but to sit very still, there wasn't much entertainment. The choir and the minister. Ho hum. So I had to invent things to amuse myself.

This involved imagination. If you looked up — up so far your hat almost fell off, only the elastic under your chin holding it in place, there was a round window — above Walt, above the choir. This window was comprised of sections of coloured glass — red and blue and white. It looked like a pie. I spent hours imagining the flavours of that pie, especially since the different segments would have different flavours. Blue would be blueberry, red would be partridgeberry and white maybe *blanc mange*. I remember thinking once that the red could be Jell-O, but then quickly dismissed it, as it would be silly to have a Jell-O pie.

I had to wear gloves to church even in the summer when it was warm. White summer gloves. That was the only place to wear them — to church. Avon made a children's cologne called *Daisies won't tell*. I had a bottle on my dresser, and dabbed some of that on me before I went to church. The adults wore Yardley's,

Evening in Paris, and Avon fragrances such as Topaz and Here's my Heart. I could hardly wait to wear grown-up fragrances.

I was allowed to wear good jewellery to church such as my gold locket, but not junk jewellery. I collected the latter with great zeal, including a bracelet with dangly little red and blue drops, not unlike the colours of that favourite window in the church. So, before leaving the house, I would surreptitiously slip on the bracelet, and then stuff it inside my white glove so that it didn't show. Once seated beside my Mother in church, I'd pull the bracelet out over my glove and adjust my hat at the back, so the people behind us could see it. Then stuff it back underneath the glove before my Mother could catch me, if I was lucky.

Church became way more interesting after I joined Junior Choir. The choir loft was like a spy loft. You could see everything!

The choir ante-rooms were accessed from the back of the church. There was a door from the outside leading into the ante-room, and an inside door and steps which led to your side of the choir loft. The men's ante-room had two inside doors — one for the choir members which had steps leading to their side of the choir loft and the other for the minister which led directly into the sanctuary.

While waiting for the processional hymn, you could

peek underneath the seats in the choir, and get an obstructed view of who was coming into the church. This was a rather delicious thing to do — it felt very spy-like and sneaky.

Having taken your seats in the choir, it was a free-for-all gawk. Change of season was the most interesting time because there was a parade of new togs, which you couldn't wait to get home and match up in the catalogues. Summer was particularly entertaining, because in addition to the regular folks, there were people from Away who were visiting. They arrived on a steamer or boat from somewhere, sometimes having travelled long distances. One such visitor stands out in my memory. It was probably late '50's or 1960, early in my career as Junior Choir member. Sandwiched between Nanc and Shirl in Junior Choir I looked out in the congregation and saw a woman whose clothes could not be exactly matched to the items offered in that year's Simpson's and Eaton's catalogues. Similar, but not an exact replica. And, I might add, the most extreme of those fashions. The hat resembled a science-fiction space ship — huge orbital brim with a small crown section for the head. A pastel floppy topper with one big button at the throat complemented the hat. But the *pièce de resistance* were the shoes — high spiky heels and pointed toes. How she walked over the pebbly rocks is anybody's guess. But we weren't about to miss out on a close-up view.

The benediction barely out of the minister's lips — we flew at breakneck speed out the choir ante-room door, over the rocks and down to the front door. We got up those front steps just in time to witness the heel of one of those shoes crashing through a seam in the wooden porch. Now *there* was something to talk about when we got home.

We weren't allowed to chew gum in church, or eat candy. You could possibly be forgiven for a Vick's cough drop if you had a bit of a cold. What you were allowed was Sen-Sen. Teeny-tiny flat black squares that came in a little paper envelope, which you could dispense between the pages of your hymnary, and access as needed. Sen-Sen were small in size but unmatched in intensity. The flavour was strong — a cross between liquorice and medicine. It would clear sinuses, mask foul breath, mitigate boredom in a long sermon, and tune up vocal chords before singing. They cost 5 cents per envelope — perhaps one of the most cost-efficient products ever invented.

The bell rang twice before a service — the first about a half-hour before the start of a service, and the last one just five or ten minutes before it started.

Obadiah rang the bell. He was a stocky gentleman with one arm. (He had lost the other arm as a young man in a rifle mishap.) I thought he was amazingly clever to be able to navigate the ropes and the bell tower with one arm. In actual fact, he was also wharf master. Legend has it that Obadiah single-handedly (no pun intended) and routinely cleaned the oil lamps lining each side of the church in the days before generator power (which preceded my generation). The oil lamps still sat in the brackets on the walls — preserving a sense of history for those of us who were younger, and evoking pleasant memories for the older generation who had experienced the lamps as part of their evening vespers.

On the wall underneath the male side of the choir was a granite plaque. It looked like a tombstone from the graveyard, but instead it was mounted on the wall. It stated, "*In loving memory of URIAH STARKES who gave 44 years of faithful service to this church*" or something to that effect. I thought of Uriah Starkes as Moses — a religious heavyweight. He was dead before I was born but since I shared his surname, I sort of thought of myself as a Nipper's Harbour Uriahite (as in Israelite). I felt rather proud and important when I contemplated that tombstone plaque.

Upstaging the change of season, in terms of observational fodder, was a change in minister. Especially if that minister had kids. The old United Church manse was a large two-story building so it could accommodate ministers with large families. The minister we had when I was in Grades 1 and 2 had a daughter who was in my classroom, and she was a wild one! Two characteristics stand out in my mind about this kid, and they have to do with her hands. I don't remember what she looked like, but her hands are clear as a bell. Pink nail polish smeared rather crudely on her nails. And cod liver oil capsules, which she squirreled away (obviously avoiding swallowing them) and when she got to school she would snap them. Gross! Cod liver oil smeared all over her hands. I used to think of her as blubber barrel — a rather un-Christian and uncharitable sentiment. But really, it was bad enough to have to get through the summer with those blubber barrels **rendering out** in the **stages**, without having this youngster smearing it all around school. In retrospect, I think of how hard it must have been for her to fit into her new environment. And perhaps this was her way of letting us know she was no "goody-two- shoes" minister's kid.

The ministers, who often stayed about four years, came from different parts of the island, so it was interesting to observe the different accents — easily done, given the oratorical responsibilities of their job. There were a couple of Reverends whose roots were in the Bonavista/Trinity Bay area. Their speech was riddled with those soft sounds — e.g. harbour was *hawbaw* — this Bostonian-like drawl was pleasant enough. It made sermons more bearable.

There was another church in Nipper's Harbour known as the Church of England then, referred to later as Anglican. It was the oldest church — a small, quaint and charming wooden structure in a protected nook in the harbour. Whereas Nipper's Harbour was the nucleus of the pastoral charge for the United Church (the minister went to the other points on his charge by boat or dog-team), Nipper's Harbour was one of the outposts of the Church of England Diocese. Therefore services at that church were intermittent. And most of their parishioners attended services at the United Church when their priest wasn't there.

Likewise, when there was something big going on in the Church of England, such as a visit from the Bishop or the Lieutenant-Governor, many of the United Church members honoured the occasion by attending. It was on one of these occasions that Nanc, Shirl and I — the mighty trio — went to observe and participate. I was about seven or eight years old at the time. We sat at the back and struggled with the liturgy — you needed your engineering papers to navigate that prayer book. When it was all over, we filed out and had to shake hands with the visiting dignitary. This is the part where I got rattled — having survived the formality and ritual of the highly liturgical service, this was the final piece. My heart racing and feeling quite insignificant, I stuck out my left hand. The visiting dignitary said "Left hand, that's the way the Girl Guides do it". I knew immediately I had goofed, and that he was attempting to rescue me. I was mortified. Furthermore, Nanc and Shirl were witnesses to this *faux pas* and would never let me live it down.

The experience of church in Nipper's Harbour was a positive one. Aside from my own spiritual development, a life-long journey, I learned many other aspects of life. For example, the significance of ritual and ceremony, the value of community, and respect of difference. These values have helped define who I am, have informed my choices, and have helped me live successfully in community with the many twists my life has taken.

The Old Cemetery

A stone's throw from Sterling's shop, and on the path to the lookout was the old cemetery. It was fenced in, unused, and overgrown with weeds. There were headstones with people's names, dates of birth and death and small epitaphs — the same as in the new cemetery, as far as I could tell. But that was only what you could see from outside the fence.

Because we knew we were not to step foot inside that fence. How did we know? Our parents had told us first of all, but also because there are just some things you knew you were not supposed to do. For instance, you were not to go down on the breakwater and jump overboard. And you were not ever to set foot inside the old cemetery.

It was very different from the new cemetery in that regard. Because not only did we attend funerals and burials in the new cemetery, but also sometimes on a Sunday afternoon in the summer, after we had finished our big mid-day Sunday dinner, after the dishes were washed and put away, we would take a leisurely stroll over to Welsh's Cove to pay our respects to the dead. And without fail, there would be other families doing the same thing. The liveliest place in Nipper's Harbour on a summer's Sunday afternoon was the cemetery.

The difference between the two cemeteries, as far as I could determine, was that most of the people who died and were buried in the old cemetery, had suffered from diphtheria (which we called *dipteria* in Nipper's Harbour). And when it was talked about, it sounded like the Black Plague in Europe. The headstones were old — many of them from the 1800's, and some were children's graves, marked by small headstones. I supposed there must have been an epidemic and they dropped like flies. And it had such an impact on the community that many generations later, we still were not going to that cemetery.

Sometimes, after going to Sterling's shop and buying some candy, we would walk by that old cemetery. Sucking on my peppermint knob, and peering through the pickets of that fence, I'd wonder aloud to Nanc or Shirl, (the founts of all knowledge as far as I was concerned), why we couldn't go in. They were quick to respond that if we went in there we would get diphtheria and die. It really would be just as foolish as diving off the breakwater.

The old cemetery was symbolic. In a coastal community where there were so many natural elements you could not control, where fishermen lost their lives at sea, and the force of nature was ever-present, the old cemetery represented the containment of danger. It was as if diphtheria itself was buried in the cemetery. And if one of us kids opened the gate to go in, we would unleash the demon on ourselves and everyone else. It speaks to how terrible the whole epidemic must have been. If the tombstones could talk, one can only imagine what the story would be.

The old cemetery is still there. It has always served as a landmark. People referenced it every day in conversation. "I walked up to the lookout and took the old cemetery path." It was integrated into the everyday fabric of life.

And the souls that died were sort of like the war-dead. They had fought a battle and laid down their lives for the rest of us.

Every time I hear the word diphtheria, I think of the old cemetery. And remember in my child's mind that diphtheria no longer exists, because it's buried in that famous landmark.

Christmas Celebrations

*Every year when I hear that first Christmas carol, or
Bing's old pipes crooning "I'll be home for Christmas",
I want to bawl. It always hits me out of the blue – I could
be racing through the Rideau Centre, headed for Shopper's
Drug Mart to get something as mundane as Head &
Shoulders shampoo on sale, and boom! Lumps the size of
tennis balls grab my throat, and the waterworks start
pouring down my face. My knee-jerk reaction is anger –
anger that "they" are abusing my emotions this way,
especially if I didn't remember to put a Kleenex in my
pocket, and have to find the washroom to get some toilet
paper, or in the worst-case scenario use my sleeve. This is
immediately followed by sadness, and ultimately after a
little self-talk, joy. Ah yes, the sadness. The ghosts of
Christmases past. The loss of loved ones who were such
a rich part of that past, but paradoxically the joy they
have left in my heart just by having been here.*

*Nipper's Harbour, where I experienced my first
Christmases, represents for me a classic drama, richer
than Dicken's <u>A Christmas Carol</u> with Alistair Simms.*

T he first inkling of Christmas started in the very
early years around September. That's when
Eaton's and Simpson's Christmas catalogues
came out. In later years it got earlier and earlier in the
summer, which kind of ruined the flow of things. It
was brutal if both Simpson's and Eaton's catalogues
arrived on the same day. We lived in the cove; the post
office was in the harbour. Shirl and I each had several
people's mail to collect — Shirl had her Mom's, Nan's,
and Great Aunt Mim's. I had the mother lode — Mom,
Grandma, Aunt Mabel and Aunt Muriel. Nanc had
only her mother's. So by the time we got to the 72-
steps and ascended less than half-way up, our poor
little arms sore from toting, we sat down, ripped off
that brown paper outer wrapper, and let our eyes feast
on the wonders of those first few pages. Part of the
excitement was seeing the catalogue before anyone
else. Shirl and Nanc and I prided ourselves on knowing
stuff — took courage from it, maybe even a sense of
smugness, self-possession.

More than the catalogue, snow was the link to the
magic of Christmas. So the one year we didn't get snow

by Christmas Eve, the adults created magic for the kids by having Santa arrive in Randall's Cove by passenger boat. That was really something. We were forewarned that Santa had a bit of transportation challenge going on, and the local men were doing all in their power to ensure he was able to get to Nipper's Harbour. And he did. There he was — jolly old St. Nick in his red suit and white beard, jingling his sleigh bells, dismounting from Uncle Lo's passenger boat. The magic could happen — snow or no snow. Every year, they never let us down.

Christmas Eve was the most fantastic event of the year in Nipper's Harbour. It happened in the Orange Lodge. There was a huge tree. Gifts were tied to the tree. What an amazing sight! There was a meal prepared in homes and brought to the Orange Lodge. For those in the cove, food and gifts were brought by boat, unloaded at the Union Store wharf and carried up the hill. Salads, meats, homemade bread and pickles and beets. But the best — desserts of every description — was the beginning of the Christmas dazzle. Decorated cakes with sparkles and sprinkles, and candy, and cookies of all kinds. Those formed into the shape of strawberries, with leaves made from green icing were my favourite. It must have taken hours to make, and we gobbled them up in glee as we waited for the rest of the events to unroll.

The year I was in Grade One we had a fabulous

Christmas concert. We were dressed in white crepe paper outfits, representing popcorn, and popped out of the ante-rooms onto the stage singing:

> *The popcorn pops and it pops out white*
> *A yummy little fellow that we like to bite*

But the role in this drama I envied, and would never have, belonged to Brenda, a petite little girl, also in Grade One, who sang a solo, after we had done our cavorting around the stage. It went like this:

> *Don't forget me, don't forget me*
> *I may be small, I may be wee*
> *But please, please, please*
> *Don't forget me.*

My genes and appetite prevented me physically from ever landing a 'dying swan' role, but it sure had a lot of appeal.

So, here we were in the old Orange Lodge, with the wood stove throwing off heat, the tables laden with food for a sit-down meal, the Christmas tree sharing the stage with a Christmas concert by the school youngsters, and the anticipation of Santa arriving at the end of the evening for distribution of the gifts. And thrown in the middle of all those going-ons was my Great Aunt Nellie making homemade ice cream for us kids in a manual ice-cream maker.

Just to build the excitement for the children waiting for Santa Claus, sometimes a telegram would arrive from Rudolph, which would be read from the stage, indicating the status of Santa's whereabouts. For instance, one year the telegram stated that Santa and the reindeer were tangled in Cliff's woodpile in Burton's Pond, and as soon as they had cleared that obstacle, they would be along. This brought great laughs from the adults, but made us kids kind of nervous. When would he ever get here?

As if we hadn't had magic enough, the walk home with my Dad was sometimes the best of all. My Mom would stay behind with the women to clean up — I suspect they were there until quite late. Then the walk home through the snow — up the 72-steps and down to the cove, being guided by the star-lit sky. There was no electricity and no streetlights. This set the stage for the religious part of Christmas, with the star guiding the three Wise Men to Jesus.

The next night, the night of the 25th, members of the church and community would traipse around the whole outport singing Christmas carols to the sick and shut-in. Musical accompaniment was usually a piano accordion, played by Pleman Rideout, one of the organists at church. His fingers freezing in the frosty air, he squeezed out the bars of "Silent Night" and "O Little Town of Bethlehem" with relative ease. We usually gathered outside the living room window of the house we were serenading, and admired the lights from the tree and wreaths as we sang. And without fail, at the end of the carol, the door would open, and a hand would emerge with a fresh box of Pot of Gold chocolates, which would be passed around to the carollers. By the end of the night, our voices were strained; our feet and noses cold, but our blood sugars had reached an all-time high.

The Christmas Story — the reason for all these festivities — was repeated every year at church and Sunday School. Mary, Joseph and the baby Jesus, the Shepherds, the Wise Men, the donkey, the manger, all figured prominently. Bible readings, Sunday School programs and carol sing-a-longs ensured we knew what we were preparing for — the twelve days of Christmas.

It was an extended party. There were activities which took place from Christmas Day until January 6th referred to as "Old Christmas Night", which did not happen any other time of year.

One of these activities was mummering, referred to by some as "jannying", and others as "dressing up". The Newfoundland Dictionary describes a mummer as "an elaborately costumed and disguised person who participates in various group activities at Christmas".

It goes on to say, quoting from <u>Mummering in New-foundland (1969)</u> — "Both the 'little mummers' and 'big mummers' give the same cue before entering a house: they knock on the door, and give an ingressive shout (that is, they draw in their breath) while saying, 'mummers allowed?' Once inside, they begin a jogging, half-dance, half-shake that is the "mummer's walk".

Because they had on disguises, including masks, which the locals referred to as false faces, there was a guessing game of who these people were. And because you knew everyone in the community, you could perhaps find clues in the clothing (if you were a keen observer with a good memory), or an inadvertent telling mannerism. But any talking was in the mummer's voice as described above. Sometimes they danced, and carried on. And sometimes it was just two or three people who sat quietly. The game was to try and get them to talk. And if you guessed who they were correctly, they were supposed to lift their "false face" — which sometimes was an old pillowcase with eyeholes cut out and held in place on the head by a hat or sou'wester or other headgear.

The mummers would arrive in waves, beginning after supper and going on until close to midnight each night. Constant entertainment. In your own home, in the kitchen.

Another activity during those twelve days was visiting

from house to house, and being invited to "have your Christmas". What was meant by that was a snack — a cup of tea or more likely a glass of Purity syrup (cherry, orange, lemon or raspberry), diluted with water, accompanied by a tea plate of goodies — light fruit cake, dark fruit cake, old cheddar (referred to as rat-trap cheese), a Purity milk lunch biscuit, and maybe a cookie or square or two.

It was as if the whole community had embarked on a twelve-day party. Everyone was participating — everyone hosting everyone else. As the days counted down to Old Christmas Night, a growing feeling of sadness enveloped us kids as we thought of returning to the mundane routine of school, homework, normal meals and normal bedtimes.

The magic was over for another year. The manifest magic. But the latent magic in our hearts stayed with us in anticipation of the next Christmas. Most importantly, we knew beyond the shadow of any doubt that we were valued — not just by our immediate families, but also by the whole community. Not only had we received but we had contributed — every carol we sang, every role we played in the Christmas concert, every mummer we let in, and every person we visited had been an important part of the whole experience.

A whole community of 350 people raised me. How rich is that? It's no wonder I get all choked up about it.

Death in an Outport

T his story is about death. It's not a morbid story, but one that reflects the inclusiveness of death as a meaningful chapter in the life cycle.

Children were not sheltered from this, but were participants in the unfolding rituals and drama that occurred in the days, weeks and months that followed populace death.

Birth, baptism, marriage and death — those were the big events in Nipper's Harbour — the life markers, associated with ceremony and protocol, involving most people in the outport. Even if not active participants in the ceremonies we all knew about them.

There were no phones. The news was passed from person to person, house to house. Maybe at the store or the post office or on Starkes' **Room** or Noble's **Room**. Sometimes my Dad would arrive home for dinner, and announce "Poor old George gave up the ghost this morning." Or "Well, Aunt Mary is gone to her great reward today." I wasn't very old when I figured out what this meant: death, wake, funeral, grave, burial, wreaths, church, cemetery, black clothes, blinds drawn.

There were no funeral parlours. The only parlours were in people's homes, and at a death these were transformed. The body was "laid out" — prepared for burial by volunteers in the outport community. It was a skill that was passed from generation to generation, and a task taken seriously and responsibly. My Great Aunt Hagar was one of them. If you saw her tearing off somewhere in the day outside her normal routines, you suspected that somebody might have died. It was very important to get the body washed and dressed for viewing before *rigor mortis* set in. Even somebody dashing off to Aunt Hagar's home could trigger alertness to what news might be coming later in the day.

Local carpenters who built boats also made the coffins. They were decorated and finished with materials from L.J. Noble & Sons. It was placed somewhat precariously on a row of chairs in the parlour and usually beside a window, which, depending on the season of the year, would be opened to promote air circulation. There was no formaldehyde or embalming fluid. There was something called "Florida water" — a sickly sweet, part floral, part citrus odour that wafted about the corpse. I don't know whether it was on the corpse or on the clothing and shroud covering the corpse, but I remember feeling a bit wheezy by the smell. Too much exposure could even make you a bit heavish.

Previous generations had firsthand experiences with waking practices. People from my parents' generation told the story of being curious as kids about corpses. On one such occasion, a group of youngsters decided they would take a peek at the corpse through the window — from outside. One of the young girls climbed onto the shoulders of a boy to take a look. She still wasn't able to get a good view, so he gave her a shove. And yes, true to form the window was open, so Gladys got an up-close and personal face-to-face view of the corpse. Beating a hasty retreat, their curiosity more than satisfied, they did not repeat this practice again. But the story had a long life.

Just as there were no commercial funeral parlours and undertakers, there were no professional grave-diggers. That job went to the ablest, fittest men. The optimal time to die in Nipper's Harbour was that period in the Spring after the ground had thawed and when the men weren't yet in the throes of fishing, or late Fall just before the ground froze and after the men had taken up their fishing nets. The angel of death did not always comply with this optimum window of opportunity. Sometimes the men struggled to dig graves in the frozen earth, and sometimes in the busiest work months when most men averaged about four hours sleep per night. But what had to be done, had to be done. Off to Welsh's Cove (the site of both cemeteries — Anglican and United) with picks and shovels. I don't know, but sometimes I imagined how that might have been. Because it was getting awfully crowded in that old United Church (previously Methodist) cemetery, family plots had the members lined up cheek-by-jowl so to speak, and that's what I used to wonder about, but was too chicken to ask. Did they ever see any skeletons or disintegrated coffins when they dug the holes? If they did, they looked after it before the public got there. Every grave hole I ever peered into looked clean as a whistle. But secretly it was always suspect.

But I'm getting ahead of myself. Before the burial were the wake and the funeral. As children we were sort of protected from actually going to see the dead. That was more or less an adult activity. (Thus Gladys' curiosity getting the better of her in my earlier reference). But we were allowed and even encouraged to go to funerals.

Funerals were sombre, deadly affairs. Dressed up in your Sunday clothes, off you went. Usually I was with my Mom and aunts. Because my Dad and or uncles were often pallbearers or gravediggers or both. Or if the deceased was not a close relative, and it was the middle of summer, they could be working.

What I remember is the solemness of sitting in the church waiting for the whole deal to start. You had to be even more quiet and still than was expected in a Sunday service. No whispering, no movement or shuffling or wriggling about. And, like the deceased, you were barely allowed to breathe.

The tolling of the bell broke the dreadful silence. Each deadly thud made my heart race faster and faster. And then the intoning of the minister reciting *Jesus said,* 'I am the resurrection and the life.' We all stood. The minister, the pallbearers carrying the coffin, and the mourners all filed in. The front centre pews were cordoned off for the mourners. They sat for the whole ceremony. We were up and down, up and down, same as Sundays. Except it was dreadfully sombre. Very sombre Bible readings, sad mournful hymns and prayers that droned on.

Draped on top of the casket, sometimes arranged around the floor if there was superabundance, were wreaths and sprays and artificial flowers. Bought at L.J. Noble & Sons, the wreaths were from the immediate family members and close friends, while sprays, cheaper and smaller, came from the more disconnected. It was a formula, of sorts.

Then on our feet again for the procession out. The pallbearers had black armbands on the arms that bore the casket. What a job. There were three sets of descending steps from the United Church to the cove, then up a hill and across a meadow to Welsh's Cove.

All the houses en route to the cemetery had their blinds pulled down as the procession passed. Just as the blinds of the family members of the deceased had been down since the person died and would not be up until the day after the funeral.

We quietly walked to the gravesite, where there were more prayers that droned on and a hymn. One of the favourites being "Shall we gather at the river".

Shall we gather at the river
The beautiful, the beautiful, the river.
Gather with the saints at the river
That flows by the throne of God.

Mmm. A bit confusing. Here we were in the jaws of the Atlantic Ocean. Welsh's Cove was actually quite beautiful. And the dead were going to hang out with saints?? At a river?? A muddy old creek? Either God had poor taste in his throne location, or there was something dreadfully wrong here. Couldn't question that either. That would have been considered disrespectful and sacrilegious. Thank God one always had the freedom to think, if not to speak.

The *pièce de résistance* at those burial rites was when the L.O.B.A. was involved. The Loyal Orangemen and Women dressed in their regalia. The women wore white dresses and ornamental sashes, and the men had even larger ornamental sashes. And if one of their members happened to be the deceased, they had a ritual they performed at the graveside. Something to do with ribbons pinned onto their lapels that in chorus became unpinned and dropped one by one on top of the casket as they circled it before it was lowered into the ground. They did their own little speech and prayers and things before the minister picked up a handful of loose earth and, sprinkling it on the casket, finished off with "Ashes to ashes, dust to dust".

So, I'm thinking perhaps the Orangemen and women types had a jumpstart in a place on the river. What was all that about anyway? Another story, another time.

It was another slice of life, the whole death and funeral thing in Nipper's Harbour. But a critically important piece of my development. Realities of life and death, and the use and meaning of ceremony to make some sense of the mystery of it all.

Sunday School Picnics

*I*t wasn't as exciting as Christmas Eve in the Orange Hall, but it was definitely a runner-up. The annual Sunday School Picnic — in the summer, of course.

It was more than a picnic. It was an event. Before the good stuff — the games, the candy toss and the actual food in Welsh's Cove, before we put on our play clothes, there was the serious part of the picnic.

We had a parade. All the Sunday School children dressed up in their Sunday clothes — for Nanc and Shirl and I this meant our Sunday dresses, ankle socks and good shoes, and marched around to the sick and shut-ins to sing hymns. Because it had to be a fine day, which usually meant an ocean breeze, we had the tricky task of keeping our dress tails in place with one hand and hanging onto our hymnaries with the other. This was not our most favourite part of the day.

All the old people would smile and nod in appreciation from their doorways, or if it was fine they might even sit outside for the serenade. Unlike carolling, no-body passed around a box of chocolates after these hymns. It wasn't chocolate season.

We sang "Abide with me", "The Lord is my Shep-herd", and other old-people's hymns. I think we even did "Jesus loves me" and "Jesus bids us shine" — old familiar Sunday-school tunes. Our hearts really weren't into this part of the drill. We couldn't wait to get to Welsh's Cove.

My Great Grandmother chose this occasion to make her grand exit to the great beyond. Carried to the sky on the sound of our cherubic little voices singing hymns. It was the usual drill — a sunny, windy day in July. I was wearing my mint-green chiffon Sunday dress, strug-gling with the tail in the wind, sandwiched between Nanc and Shirl. We were anticipating the fun part of the afternoon after all this singing was over.

My Great Grandmother, her usual cheerful self, was sitting on a chair on the front porch, smiling and nodding at this one and that one as we prepared to sing. She had gotten dressed up for the occasion — although she wore navy blue dresses all the time. This was a good navy blue dress, and her lace-up oxfords for comfort and stability. Roy Andrews, the son of Walt, the church organist, and musical like his father, was doing the accompaniment on a piano accordion. Every-thing was going along nicely, the music, the singing, the wind, our dress tails, and the occasional baa from Sterling's sheep, when we heard a thud. The music and singing stopped, adults ran to the front porch. Now in her 90's, this was obviously more excitement than Great Grandmother could handle.

Usually, the Sunday School parade went off without this much drama. That was a unique year, the year Great Grandmother died. I was between the ages of seven and eight years, and it was my first experience with death.

But...on to Welsh's Cove, where the party went on. There were games and candy tosses for the children. L. J. Noble & Sons, and I suspect the Union Store as well, donated candy for the candy toss. The trouble was that the big kids got the big haul on this. I was an only child and had no clue how to compete on a physical level. I just stood there and waited for candy to land at my feet. Wrapped candy — mostly English toffee, but also Purity kisses. It was like manna from heaven. I would wonder if that's what God tossed down to the Israelites when they were wandering around in the dessert with nary a bite to eat. Wrapped candy — that was surely the most sanitary thing to toss out on the ground. "Manna" was some generic, non-specific term with no terms of reference. Therefore, it must have been wrapped English toffee. It was amazing what you could figure out when you took the time to think about it.

Welsh's Cove was the most level place in Nipper's

Harbour. The fact that the Anglican and United Church cemeteries shared this space did not detract from the party atmosphere of the Sunday School Picnic. The fact that both the cemeteries and the picnic were associated with the church more or less made them level playing fields. There was plenty of space for families to spread blankets and tablecloths for the feast.

Nothing was ever done on a small scale in Nipper's Harbour. Dishes were packed for this outdoor meal — ones you had to wash when it was all over and you went home. The only paper products used were serviettes, and these were usually floral with gold-coloured gilded edges. The food was packed in containers. My Mom's picnic basket/tin was plaid with yellow handles. It was large enough to hold the cold cooked chicken legs, potato salad, beet salad, pickles, homemade bread and butter, squares and fruitcake. Thermoses of tea and jugs of Purity syrup mixed with water were toted separately.

The notion of being outdoors and eating while sitting on the ground was quite liberating. Fortunately my Mother shared my views on this *al fresco* experience. Sometimes in the summer when my Dad was out in the boat, she made sandwiches and lemon crystals mixed with sugar and water, and she and I would go up to the lookout. It was almost like mini Sunday School picnics.

Meanwhile, back at the real event, there was a lot of celebration and laughter. People visited with each other, sometimes sharing each other's food, hamming it up for photographs, finding an odd toffee in the grass that the kids had missed. The laughter and lyrical cadence of the voices ricocheted off the surrounding cliffs. The joyfulness was contagious. It was a happy event — well except for that one year when my Great Grandmother checked out.

It was before the road, before the sound of car motors and car horns, before the landscape had been monkeyed with. The sound of human voices and seagulls and the odd crow of a rooster settled into your soul and took root, and took form. So it was more than the event itself. In an odd sort of way, it was a spiritual experience, although the appreciation of this aspect would not become a conscious awareness until fifty years later.

The Scratches

*T*hat day in Nipper's Harbour in the summer of 1957 — standing in the line-up with my Mother who had a firm grip on my hand, waiting my turn for the TB vaccine, known locally as "the scratches".

The *Christmas Seal* was in port — a medical boat which offered x-rays to adults, and whose staff set up a clinic in the Anglican school to provide TB vaccine to the kids. I knew it was important, not only because of my Mother's sweaty grip on my hand. But I sensed nervousness and tension from my Mother. It's that sixth sense that pre-schoolers have before it gets contaminated by life on the planet. As a four-year- old, I didn't know, nor at that age could I have understood, that the kids my Mom had gone to school with, in fact sat with, had died from TB. I didn't know that poor kids were more vulnerable. How was I to know that my Grandfather, a businessman, could better provide for his family than the fathers of some classmates of my Mom who died? For this reason my Mom sometimes struggled with survivor guilt. I didn't know what this pending procedure entailed, and perhaps neither did she.

What I did know is that one of the kids in the line-up ahead of me — Stevie Owl — was screaming blue murder. Blood-curdling, lung-bursting howls ricocheting off the walls of that old Anglican school, cum TB clinic, on that rare hot summer's day. Plaintive, residual whimpers emanated from Stevie's little lips as he left, commenting to his mother, "Some dood, Mommie, iddin it?" Stella, my Mother, tightened the grip on my small hand. Terror took over in my gut. There was no escape.

As it got closer to my turn, the smell of rubbing alcohol and antiseptic overwhelmed me, and before I knew it, two white-capped strapping nurses grabbed my fear-frozen body and whipped me onto a table, turned me over, pulled down my pants, and inflicted three or four subcutaneous scratches across my backside. It stung. I couldn't see it. Fear, pain and rage engulfed me. Not to be outdone by any boy, and with a good pair of lungs myself, I set out to surpass Stevie Owl in the volume department. And I threw in some physical resistance for good measure. Other adults were enlisted to help hold me down. At some point I stopped struggling — perhaps the soft bandage application over the wounds was a signal that the worse was over.

The long walk back to our house in the cove was anti-climactic. I peppered my relieved and embarrassed Mother with a four-year-old's questions. How long is that bandage going to be on my bum? Who's going to take it off? You, or those nurses? Will it hurt? Why is it still stinging now? When will it stop? Can I have a bath? By the time we had navigated all the higgledy-piggledy rocks and mounds surrounding the school and had scaled the 72-steps climb up the cliff before the descent to our house, I had sort of forgotten the whole ordeal.

I was anxiety-ridden, trying to get my practicum squared away – the last requirement for my graduate degree in Social Work from the University of Toronto. So few spaces up for grabs. Finally, I was matched with North York General Hospital – survived the screening interviews, and just had to complete the organizational red tape. This included medical tests, blood work, x-rays. Summoned to the medical office for follow-up, I wondered what sinister disease was sitting dormant in my active, agile body. "Ms. Starkes, you tested positive for TB", said the ashen-faced staff health nurse. Shocked! Tuberculosis! 1983 it was. TB had been virtually eradicated in Canada. Then it came flooding back, like one of those old National Film Board black and white documentaries.

So there I was decades later, face to face with the Staff Health Nurse from North York General. "I had a TB vaccine" I stammered, "when I was a kid." Those Ratchet-like nurses obviously did a good job — since the inoculation was still going strong in my bloodstream. "You must have been born in Newfoundland or Saskatchewan" was the staff nurse's reply. The provinces most at risk for a TB epidemic. She kindly offered me a verification certificate to carry in my wallet, preventing future fiascos and unnecessary frights. A few years after graduating from the University of Toronto I visited a friend, a fellow Newfoundlander who had married a Californian. Sitting on her living room floor in Pasadena late one night, we were having a glass of wine and getting caught up. At that stage in my life I had commenced electrolysis to remove unwanted facial hair. My friend who had also been unblessed with fair skin and dark hair asked earnestly whether this procedure was painful. "What's it like?" she said. I reflected for a second and then thoughtfully responded with "the scratches". We both broke into gales of laughter. "Where do you call it up from?" she asked. "Ah," I said, "but you do remember, don't you?"

Steamers & Ships

My parents brought me home to Nipper's Harbour in a steamer after I was born at Twillingate Hospital. Mom said they had a stateroom. While I have no conscious recollection of this event, I enjoyed all the subsequent trips on steamers with my family. Often it was just women and kids who were travelling as passengers, because the men were fishing. Once I went to Twillingate with my Mom and Grandma and we stayed in Stockley's boarding house. I think they were there to see the doctor, but I thought the whole event was a lark.

I liked sleeping in those cots in the stateroom, and found the cardboard vomit boxes attached to each bunk to be quite the novelty. They looked like take-away Asian food boxes. I thought my Mom was joking when she explained what they were — I couldn't imagine being sea-sick. I found some other functional use for it, such as squirreling away my barrettes and crayons.

In the stateroom was also a sink with a mirror over it. While the ship rocked and rolled, I helped myself to the Noxema skin cream that either Mom or Grandma had in their toilet bag. This was after I had washed my face with Yardley's lavender soap. Then I'd comb my hair, readjust my barrettes and wonder what we were going to do next.

Eating on the steamer was at a large heavy table with heavy chairs. There's a smudgy memory of leather and wood — the leather secured to the wood with brass studs. Earthen dishes, the cup and saucer very thick — I must have had tea. The dishes had some insignia printed on them. The silverware was chunky. I suspect all these sturdy thick utensils had something to do with keeping things in place in a rocking (and rolling) environment. And the tablecloths were damp — which was rather off-putting — but it kept the dishes in place.

The Purser's office was the place that intrigued me. It seemed important. It was where the fare was paid. The Purser wore a dark uniform; the stewards wore white. It felt like we were on the Queen Mary. It was another world. Time was suspended as we cruised Notre Dame Bay to Twillingate. It was the great escape.

When steamers arrived in the middle of the night in Nipper's Harbour, the evidence for the sleeping populace was the sound of the ship's horn as it entered and left port, and the plaintive, mournful howl of Harv's dog. The wharf master, Obidiah, had to be there to tie her up, and untie her, and I suppose oversee the unloading of the freight. Perhaps some of the workers from L.J. Noble & Sons and the Union Store were also there, to receive the freight. (I don't know because this was the nocturnal period.)

Sailing ships preceded steamers. In the early 1900's, my Grandpa Starkes sailed to the Barbados and the Azores. During World War I, they were torpedoed on the Ruth Hickman, and survived with lifeboats, and a chart given to them by the Germans. In 1996, I was in a cab in Barbados, going from the airport to the dock, where I embarked on a sailing ship to cruise the Caribbean. The elderly cab driver and I got into an animated discussion, after I told him about my Grandfather. He remembered the Newfoundland salt cod, saying, "It was tick like my hand" – as he held up one thick hand to show me and drove with the other. That night we left the pier at midnight under sail, while Vivaldi's Four Seasons played on the deck. It was magical. But then, I was toting a lot of history with me – Vivaldi's Four Seasons or the howls of Harv's dog.

In the winter, there were no ships calling into port. Some winters the harbour froze over so that you could skate on it. The year I was in Grade 3 we could skate out to the islands. But the down side, no steamers. That meant no supplies. What we had, we had. What was off-loaded on the last voyage of the steamers in the Fall, had to last until the arrival of the first one in the Spring. As I recall, we actually never ran out of anything. *Au contraire*, we were usually over-supplied. This had to do with making sure you were prepared for the winter. Nipper's Harbour had the reputation of prosperity and abundance, which was renowned along the coast.

Summer was the busy steamer season and the Spring and summer had a regular schedule.

The S.S. Hopedale and the S.S. Springdale are the coastal boats I remember most. My parents talked about the S.S. Clyde with great nostalgia, but it went out of commission a long time ago. Schedules were tentative — due to winds, tides, hurricanes and other wonders of nature. The way to keep track was to listen to the Fishermen's Broadcast on the radio, which everyone did every day. The kitchen would go dead silent when the Fishermen's Broadcast came on. It was just one of those things you knew — you had to shut up to get the latest take on the winds and tides. And immediately following was the whereabouts of the steamers. It would go something like this: "The S.S. Hopedale left Bonavista at 6:00 AM this morning — expected in Lewisporte at 11:20." I would glaze over while all this was being announced on the radio — stare at the green milk jug and sugar basin on the table, the ones with the white handles. My Dad would be drinking his tea and listening intently with his ear turned in the direction of the radio. Those were the days of static. The crackly words of the announcer made it sound as if he was at sea himself — talking ship to shore.

If the steamer arrived during the day in the summer, and it was nice and sunny, and Nanc and Shirl and I were out gadding about, we would make a bee-line for the government wharf at the sound of the ship's horn. People stood on the steps leading down to the government wharf — mostly teenagers and children, but sometimes a couple of adults as well. As a general rule, people didn't go and watch the steamer, but it was sort of acceptable for kids to do this. I tore home and told my Mother everything I saw, so for her, it was almost as good as being there.

It was most fun if people were coming down the gangplank — visitors from Away. And it would be of interest if people were getting on, but they were the locals like yourself, so no big excitement there. Then there were the people on deck who were not getting off. They were looking at us looking at them. This is where I saw nuns in habits for the first time. Not being a Catholic community, I had no frame of reference for this. We had subscriptions to Life magazine and The Family Herald, but I had never seen anything like this.

They looked a bit like the Klu Klux Klan, which I had seen in magazines, or mummers, which I did know about. It would take a while to sort out all of this.

If the steamer came in and there was nobody to speak of on the deck, nobody getting on or off and not much freight, it was just a waste of time. And I had nothing exciting to report to my Mother when I went home for dinner. It was on one such occasion that I fabricated a yarn – just because I was bored. A widower in Nipper's Harbour had recently married a woman from another outport. I told my Mother I saw them getting on the steamer – going away on a honeymoon. My Mother's eyes widened with interest. I had her full attention. So I made up the details as I went along – what she was wearing, what he was wearing, how they walked up the gangplank, what their luggage was like, and who was there to see them off. That night, my Mom's friend Gladys, came over for a yarn and a cup of tea. I was ostensibly playing or reading in another room in the house, with one ear cocked to the kitchen, because this was a rich occasion to pick up gossip, when I heard my Mother reciting the story I made up earlier in the day. I panicked. She had remembered every detail verbatim, but it was all wrong. I got a sinking feeling in my stomach. What had I done? And if I didn't do some quick damage control, this yarn would spread through the place like a brushfire.

I walked tentatively to the kitchen, excused myself and asked to speak with my Mother privately. "Mom," I said, "that was a fib. I made it up". She was shocked. I had never done this before. And she couldn't believe she had fallen for it.

"That young **article**!," she said to Gladys. "She made that up". She tut-tutted. My face was burning with embarrassment in the other room as I stayed completely out of the way until Gladys finished her tea and left.

So, steamers provided entertainment — real and imagined. But they were not the only ships to come into port. Even more interesting were the Portuguese salt boats. Groups of Portuguese sailors — who wore sailor outfits like Popeye, with the little round hats, and wide-legged pants, would walk all over the town while they were in port. They quickly discovered the Lookout, Jerry's Cove and Welsh's Cove. They talked flamboyantly. Sometimes, my Uncle Cyril and I would play Portuguese sailors. He'd say gibberish, and I would respond with even more emphatic gibberish. Then we would laugh and laugh and laugh.

Play

U nencumbered by an overabundance of toys, and given just enough rules to keep us safe, we in Nipper's Harbour grew up with the freedom to use our imaginations in play.[‡]

Nanc, Shirl and I spent hours verbally drafting our own scripts. It was often done with the aid of Simpson's or Eaton's catalogue, sitting on our back steps or front porch. But we could just spontaneously spring into this game — anytime, anywhere — on the Lookout, sitting on the steps of Sterling's shop, waiting for him to open up, or whenever the mood hit us. It went something like this. One of us would announce, "Let's play make-believe", and without fail, the other two would enthusiastically agree. We would then negotiate who would

---

[‡] *This was such an important part of my growing up; it makes me nervous when I see children scripted with prescribed play.*

start, perhaps remembering who went first the last time we played this, and taking it from there.

We each made up a character. For instance, Nanc might say, "My name is Averill Pearcy and I'm a nurse. I live in New York City. I'm 34 years old and I have a boyfriend, Tony. Today I'm not working, so I'm going out shopping, and this is what I'm wearing." If we were near the catalogues, that's the part where you creatively pulled together your outfit for that day. Shoes, purse, and jewellery were included in the detailed description. Truth be told, Nanc had a cousin whose name was Averill Pearcy, and who really was a nurse. And Nancy's brother's name was Tony. Easy-peasy.

There was a distinctly competitive element to the game. Because whosever turn was next, and even worse, last, had to come up with an identity and an outfit that was even more spectacular. We always managed to come up with something as the other two listened with rapt attention. We loved doing this.

In Shirl's Nan's house, upstairs, was a room, known as Aunt Dora's room. Aunt Dora was dead and gone long before we were born, and this room of hers at the top of the stairs was like a mausoleum. The door was kept closed. As far as I know, nobody ever went into this room. But once in a while on a rainy day, when we couldn't go outside to play, Shirl's Nan let Shirl and I go up to Aunt Dora's room. There was a mildewy, moth-bally smell in this shrine — and a vast collection of musty dresses, hats and shoes. There was a steamer trunk to add to the intrigue and mystery of the place. Shirl and I would try on all these clothes, and parade around the room in the too big shoes, and laugh and giggle. It was hugely funny. And we felt quite privileged, because as far as I could tell, nobody else was ever allowed in Aunt Dora's room, let alone being able to go in there and play with the stuff. Shirl's Nan loved her to bits — I suppose that was the ticket to Aunt Dora's room.

Nanc's grandfather's house — no longer lived in, but used by her family for storage, e.g. supplies for their shop — had an upstairs that we were also given exclusive use of. At least that's what we thought. We had a room up there with an old adding machine, and bits of paper where we kept track of the inventory for our pretend shop. We had play currency that was home-made. Paper money was certificates out of the bags of Cream of the West flour; coin currency was a creative combination of things — largely Coke and soda stoppers that had been flattened into 'pretend' quarters and fifty-cent pieces, and gunshot that had been hammered into nickels and dimes. We used empty boxes and cans for supplies — Corn Flakes boxes, empty fruit cans, red Purity biscuit boxes adorned our pretend shop — set up in one of our yards. Other groups of kids also had pretend shops — so we tore around buying from each other. It was the silliest thing but we obviously had embraced the notion of capitalism in a big way. Shirl, as far as I know is the only one of us kids who chose a career in finance — and this is where she got her start, the basics in economics in our pretend shop.

Other role-playing games included playing school, playing church, and playing nurse.

Playing church was most effectively executed on our back steps. If you were organist you went to the top step, with your back to the rest, and used the landing as your pretend organ. A little further down was the minister, with back to the organist, and facing the congregation below. Everyone always wanted to be the organist, because it was fun to pretend you were playing the organ, and bop around pretending you were Walt.

Playing school was serious — the older kids always played teacher because they knew more. It was sometimes more demanding than actual school. My first career as a Kindergarten/Grade One teacher gave me a whole year to play the role of teacher. By the end of that year I had got it out of my system and moved on to something else.

I always knew Nanc would grow up to be a nurse. Not only did she assume the role of Averill Pearcy when we played make-believe, but she adored her toy nurse's kit — especially the plastic needle. As her patient, I would plead for some of the candy pills, but Nanc would invariably determine that what I really needed was a needle. She would grab the upper muscle of my arm in one hand and jab the plastic point of that needle until it made a red mark on my arm. Tears would be welling up in my eyes, but I didn't ever want to give her the satisfaction of making me bawl, so I would stiffen my quivery little lips and wait till it was over.

As an only child, I was very attached to my doll collection. I played with them mostly when I didn't have other kids to play with. I washed them, dressed them, combed their hair, washed their clothes, and at night put all 12 of them to bed, tucked them in and kissed them goodnight. They slept in the sun porch.

For washing the dolls' clothes I had a toy washing machine run by batteries that my Grandma had brought back from a trip to St. John's. When my Mom did her wash, she let me do my thing with the toy machine and my dolls clothes, which I then hung up on clothes lines which she set up for me between the kitchen table legs.

My love of baking, and appreciation of the magic, commenced with a baking kit given to me one Christmas by my Uncle Cyril. It had the little baking pans, cake mixes and sprinkles. I would sometimes make a little cake for my uncle, and deliver it to my Grandmother's house where he lived. I'd wait anxiously for him to finish his dinner, and then proudly present him with the decorated cake I had made for him. He was a horrible tease, and would often say, "Now Audrey, did you lick your fingers when you made that cake? I wonder if I've got the stomach to eat it?" Of course, he always did.

Continuing with the domestic theme, one Christmas I received a doll's house — it was two-story, with miniature furniture for the rooms. While this provided much play value, it paled in comparison with the real McCoy at the back of our house. This, in its previous life, was a house for the hens that my Mother used to keep. My Mom having dispensed with this hobby, the house was transformed into a doll's house for me. It was the envy of all my friends, and pretty soon the older kids had taken it over. Sometimes they wouldn't even let me in to play. And being as I had no clue how to fight, I let them be and found something else to do.

Outdoor games usually involved whatever kids happened to be hanging around. My favourite was hopscotch. The best time was after it rained, and the ground had partly dried off. Taking an old rusty nail, you could draw the perfect hopscotch pattern into the moist soil. You might find the remains of a previous game and simply retrace it with the nail. Then throw the nail onto that first square, hop on one leg to the second, turn around and pick up the nail, and proceed to the end. If the soil was too wet, it would be slippery, and with all that hopping and jumping there was a very good chance you would go sliding on your behind before the game was over.

Hide and seek was an ideal game to play in Nipper's Harbour because there were so many places to hide. Rocks, cliffs, overturned dories, nooks and crannies galore offered unlimited possibilities. The same could be said for cops and robbers, although girls only got to play this when there weren't enough boys to make up a team. Shirl had a younger brother who had guns and holsters. The guns had caps that would fire and smoke came out. Very cool. We would hide behind the cliffs and be ready to fire. Or just fire anyway because those caps were quite fun.

"Andy-Hover" (hand me over) was played with a small rubber ball. The only place this was ever played as far as I can recall was over Tite's house. I think the game was invented by teenage boys, who had other designs on that abandoned old house. The family had moved long before I was born – to the U.S. I think. And the house had been simply abandoned with nobody living in it or caring for it. One group of kids stood on one side of the house. Whoever had the ball shouted "andy-hover" – and let her rip. Whoever caught the ball on the other side, got to throw it back.

The older boys ransacked the inside of that old house. One day two of them found a piece of wood, and balanced it on the windowsill of an upstairs bedroom. With one of them on either end they had an improvised seesaw. Aunt Suse happened to have dropped in to visit my Mom that day and looked out the window to observe this transgression. "Those **bloomian** boys", she tut-tutted, as she folded her arms over her ample bosom, and shook her head.

Games at church socials were more civilized than the goings-on outdoors. After the meal was finished and the tables cleared, the tables and chairs were moved back to make way for "playing games". It was actually more like square dancing, but they couldn't call it that because it contravened the Methodist teachings. Angli-cans could dance and they did, and I attended those as a teenager, and really it was just a more complex version of the "games". Someone — an adult — instructed you on the moves. The "games" we played to songs we sang such as: *King William was King George's son, all the Royal racing run*; *A Hunting we will go*; *The Grand old Duke of York*; and *We're weaving our wad malls*.

Birthday parties were occasions to play little parlour games like, "I spy", "Inka-bottle, blue-a-bottle", "Button, button, who's got the button" and "Little Sally Saucer". They were not raucous events, these genteel little parties. And the games reflected the mood of the event. They matched the little tea-party atmosphere of the gathering.

Snowy, housebound days were ideal for board games. If my friends couldn't even get to my house to play, because of the weather, then my parents were stuck with playing Snakes and Ladders, Lido, Chinese Checkers or Flinch, a card game which also doubled as Muggins. My Uncle Cyril made me a board game which was played alone — "Hi-Q" I was told. I-Q? Was it an Intelligence Quotient measure? The object of the game was to have one peg left in the centre and all the others methodically and strategically removed. Uncle Cyril taught me how to do this and I caught on quickly. He made the board with small circular indentations where gunshot pellets could be used as pegs. It was also an exercise in dexterity and patience. Perhaps there was a method to his madness.

On lazy summer days, sometimes we just lollygagged around a wharf. There were lots of sea-snail shells (periwinkles) stuck to the railings — we thought we could charm the snails to come out by chanting:

Snail, snail, come out of your house
The goats are in your garden.

Occasionally a tomcod or conner (blue sea-perch) would be swimming just below. If we had a piece of string and a hook, we might just catch them. Sometimes Jeanette, a kid older than I, caught them as treats for her cat.

You might be hanging out charming the snails or trying to catch a tomcod and a steamer would blow. The lolly-gagging mood would be immediately transformed into, 'let's see if we can get to the government wharf before she ties up'. Bounding up and down all the hills and steps, we'd arrive panting in the harbour.

Our parents didn't sit around wondering how to entertain us in the summer or school breaks. We seemed to figure out that quite nicely on our own. It was the gift of freedom they gave us.

One of my work colleagues once commented, that she was amazed at how, when, metaphorically speaking, a door was shut, I always managed to find another way. This was quite a useful skill especially in working with the disenfranchised. This was perhaps the gift of freedom to create that I had been given as a child.

The Coming of the Road

S tella", my Dad stated solemnly to my Mother, as he placed the phone receiver in its cradle, "Walt is going to be **keeled**". This was following an intense phone exchange with Walt, where my Father was clarifying for Walt that you stopped at a red light and proceeded through on a green one. It had been a while now since Walt, my Dad and the other men had bought cars, and acquired driver's licenses (in that order).

There were no streetlights on the Baie-Verte Peninsula where the bulk of the driving took place. But Walt had now reached the stage where he thought he would drive to St. John's where his daughter lived. There was one traffic light to navigate on the seven or eight-hour drive to the outer limits of St. John's and that was on the Trans-Canada Highway going through Grand Falls in Central Newfoundland. That's what Walt was phoning my Dad about.

Men who had varying degrees of skill in sea navigation were adapting those skills to driving cars. Aside from the omission of a compass on the dashboard, and a rope to tie her on when arriving at a destination, they treated the car like a boat. They used the same terminology — "back aft" for the rear dashboard, "forward" for the front, and truth be known, they probably used port and starboard in their own minds, but restrained themselves from saying it out loud. They also treated the steering wheel like a tiller. They rolled with the bumps on the road like they did with the waves on the ocean, but the buoyancy factor and tide variables were all missing. So this translated into jerky driving.

Car salesmen descended on Nipper's Harbour like bees to honey as soon as the highway reached the outskirts of the community. Our reputation was one of prosperity, and here was their opportunity to cash in. And cash in they did. These fishermen would have never bought anything on credit — the whole notion was considered almost sinful. They bought the cars — new cars, with cash. Top of the line Chryslers and Fords — to be driven on a road that was not much more than boulders covered in dirt.

By Easter of that First Year of Cars, my parents and I went on a family trip to La Scie — an outport town about an hour's drive away, but it took us much longer. First was the navigation difficulty of the eleven miles of connector bedrock boulders to the main road. My Mother got out of the car at regular intervals to move some of the more sinister looking rocks. We were going so slowly, my Father hardly needed to stop for her to get out. My role was to sit in the front seat with my Dad on this trip. I was to hold a huge flashlight that I was to shine on his feet in the event we were driving in the dark. He was concerned about finding the brake pedal in an emergency in the dark. Unbelievably we made the journey there and back in one piece.

Family trips before this had always been in boat. These trips were always planned around weather reports, usually on a calm sunny Sunday in the summer. Having checked the sky, the barometer, and listened to the Gerald S. Doyle Fishermen's Broadcast on the radio on a Saturday night, we would tentatively plan to go to Harry's Harbour to visit my aunt the next day. There were no phones to let her know we were coming. Another quick look at the sky and the barometer on a Sunday morning, and off we would go. Although it was only about one hour in motor boat, my Mother always packed a lunch, and we took blankets in the event it had breezed up a bit for the journey home. The summer visits to my aunt were deliriously delicious. Sitting in the open motorboat on a calm sunny day watching the coastline move slowly by, the occasional iceberg floating past, is about as idyllic as it gets. And my Dad, who couldn't swim a stroke, handling the boat with absolute ease and confidence.

Handling the car was a different story. If they were in a boat and a storm came up, they embraced the challenge of getting back to Nipper's Harbour wharf with a compass, while they grabbed the tiller and danced the limbo with the waves. The morning we were driving to Baie-Verte, the car hit black ice and we did a 360-degree turn, my Dad was speechless. The compass and tiller couldn't help him with this one. But he gently straightened up the car and proceeded. He was used to dealing with the unpredictable. But I noticed his breathing rhythm changed, and he scratched his head a few times — something he habitually did when he was trying to figure out a puzzle.

The roads moved us from being a quaint old English seaport, frozen in time, to a modern Canadian village with electricity, water, sewer and phones happening straight away. The changes were dizzying.

Before the road and 24-hour electricity, we had generators. Well, some people had generators, but there were quite a few older people who still used oil lamps for lighting. The generators were turned on just before dusk and turned off at 11:00 PM, and they were turned on for the women to do their washing on Monday mornings.

There was a wood-burning stove in the kitchen, and a wood and oil burning stove in the living room. A fire was lit in the kitchen stove every day of the year, including the hottest day in the summer in order to cook, boil water, and bake. The notion of electric stoves took some getting used to. The first electric stove my parents bought was a "rangette" — a two-burner stove with a little oven. My Mom treated it as a sort of hobby — experimenting with cooking and baking and vowing it didn't produce the taste of dishes cooked on the wood stove, which was true. Bread, for instance. We also had a refrigerator, electric kettle and toaster, and iron. Door-to-door salesmen were having a field day, just like the car dealers. The electric iron transformed the work of women. No longer did they have to heat irons on the stove, and the heat of the electric iron could be regulated.

The electrical timesaving devices had the greatest effect on women. Their lives were made easier, and they could manage their time in a more efficient manner. As a kid, this was not immediately noticeable to me. My dinner was on the table, as usual, and my clothes were clean and ironed as they had always been. The big difference for me was that the TV could be turned on during the day. I would try and sneak in a few minutes of TV when I came home from school for lunch. No longer restricted to "I Love Lucy", "Leave it to Beaver",

"The Beverly Hillbillies", and "The Littlest Hobo", there was a whole world of daytime TV out there.

Televisions perhaps deserve a special mention. They were decisively a factor in the transitioning of Nipper's Harbour. The first purchasers of TVs (while we were still on generator power) were hosts to the hordes and masses who didn't yet have TV, especially on Saturday night — CBC Hockey Night in Canada. I remember going to our neighbour, Callie's on Thursday night to watch "The Littlest Hobo". Callie's kids were grown up and gone and she was quite happy to have me drop in and watch the show, while she did her crocheting and knitting. People dropped in and out of each other's houses all the time anyway. The only difference with the introduction of TV was that instead of entertaining each other, as had been the long-established norm, they were now being entertained. This was the beginning of the end of self-made entertainment.

The more sceptical were concerned about how the moral norms were going to be corroded with the introduction of TV. Peyton Place was seen as ultimately risqué — and it aired on a Sunday night! The attraction of this forbidden show meant I grabbed every opportunity to see it. But compensating for the worried religious group, was the Billy Graham Crusades, and Rex Humbard, and other TV evangelists. With 24-hour electricity, all these shows were available.

My Dad's young cousins, Gerald and Ronnie, as teenagers, actually set up a quasi-phone/walkie-talkie system between each other's houses. A path and a potato garden separated their houses. However, Gerald's mother, my Great Aunt Pearl was in awe of their wizardry. The leap to actual phones after the arrival of the road went beyond their wildest dreams. Instead of tearing around to each other's houses to share news, all that was required now was the phone. For my Mom it meant being able to talk with her sisters in Toronto — separated since they were teenagers. In 1966 the world got smaller as Nipper's Harbour caught up with it.

The View from my Window

*T*he bathroom in our house faced a pebble path. On the other side of the path was a running brook, over which was a wooden bridge which led to the yard of Harv's old house. That is, the house Harv used to live in, before he moved to another house, and rented the old one. The large kitchen window in Harv's old house faced square onto our bathroom window. On our bathroom window was a venetian blind. You could open it just a smidgen and, depending on eye level from the toilet seat, could get a pretty good idea of what was going on across the way.

I spent a lot of time in the bathroom. As an only child, I didn't have to fight with siblings for access. It was the only room in the house with a lock, which gives you a sense of power as a kid. You can bar yourself in, — and bar other people out. So there.

Watching Harv's house from the bathroom window was, for me, like watching episodes of a soap opera.

Harv's old house was my own personal *Coronation Street*.

Adding to the atmosphere was Harv's old dog whose house was an old oil drum on its side, so the dog could crawl in there for shelter. Harv's version of a prefabricated shelter — Harv was a Renaissance man.

The dog could have won an Olympic medal for the most mournful howl, which had added emphasis as it ricocheted off the insides of that old drum. The dog's favourite time to howl was when a steamer came into port, or left port. When the steamer's horn blew, the dog somehow felt he had to compete for airtime, and performed his masterpiece, a soulful howl. This was often in the wee hours of the morning. I'd be sound asleep, hear the steamer, and then wait a split second for the repartee. And just as I'd settle down to go back to sleep, the same steamer would leave port and there would be a repeat performance. Despite the annoyance, the old dog became a part of the rhythm of life — almost like a relative. He was our neighbour, after all.

Back to the toilet seat, the only theatre seat I knew as a child. Harv had a grandson, Dougie, who was just a whisker bit younger than I, and whom I used to play with when we were pre-schoolers. There was a running brook and Harv made awesome wooden sailboats for Dougie that he floated down that creek. Dougie used to set those sailboats free further up the creek, then lie on his stomach on that little wooden bridge and watch them float down the stream. Through the venetian blinds I watched the drama unfold. I used to get a bit nervous, and perhaps Dougie did too when the boats went under the bridge, and he waited to catch them on the other side. I would imagine goblins under that bridge ready to do something evil to Dougie's boats. But they always reappeared, which was a relief.

It was Joey Smallwood's Resettlement Program that was responsible for some of the action. There was, what I considered then, an old couple, probably in their 50s who rented Harv's house. They were from another community, whose residents were paid to move out to cosmopolitan Nipper's Harbour. From my seat I cracked the curtain (i.e. aforementioned venetian blind) to watch the strange man and woman from away, nosh on their breakfast bacon. And nosh they did. They had thick slices of bacon with rind, which they ate with their fingers and then gnawed, pulled and plucked on that rind like it was a rubber band. Bug-eyed I would de-throne and tear out to the kitchen to report the bad table manners of the foreigners to my Mother. Otherwise this couple was rather boring; they came and went quietly.

Of course there was the constant flow of moving traffic on that pebble path. In particular, one woman commuted with great regularity with her slop-pail to the beach. She made a racket. On top of the sound of her feet hitting the pebbles, she walked with some difficulty because of bunions on her feet. They must have hurt, because she made painful little grunts with each step. And because it was not a smooth walk, the pail rattled. So as I sat there on the toilet seat, staring across the way, procrastinating my job of drying the dishes in the kitchen, hoping my Mother would get tired of waiting for me and dry them herself, I would hear the rhythmic grunt-grunt, rattle-rattle of this woman heading for the beach. Barely opening one slat of that venetian blind — just a crack, I waited for her to pass by. There were times I envisioned her and that old rattley pail going flying over the rocks. But it never happened. She and the bucket were an integrated and comfortable part of the landscape.

The fisher folk who lived up that lane walked by several times a day, commuting to and from their home and the wharf. They nattered on about the weather, the direction of the wind and the tide.

My theatre seat got greatest use the year the road came through. No sooner had the road come through, they started with the electrical system and so forth. This required the expertise of outsiders. Before I knew what had happened, Harv's old house had been temporarily rented to a worker who was there for the summer. He brought his family. I was glued to my theatre seat that summer. My parents practically had to buy tickets to get access to the bathroom.

I had by now seen the show *The Beverly Hillbillies* on TV. This family renting Harv's house was the "Newfie Hillbillies". They arrived (husband, wife and too many kids to count) in a truck piled to the rafters. They toppled out of that truck helter-skelter. Their stuff was completely disorganized. I saw a plastic dishpan, bags, boxes, stuff and youngsters flying in all directions. I was speechless. I went out to the kitchen and announced to my Mother that we were in for it. Never in my limited life had I seen such chaos. The plot would thicken over the summer.

The same kitchen table on which I had seen the couple eating their breakfast bacon in what I judged as a very uncivilized fashion, would in view of this crew, be remembered as the epitome of manners.

"Mom", I announced, "they opened up a tin of peas and plunked it on the table. Passing it around like a crowd of savages. Didn't even heat them up. What's the matter with them?" While my Mother discouraged me from being judgemental, I could tell she was interested in the details.

There was a little boy around four years old, whom I began to feel sorry for by the end of that summer. It seemed like nobody was ever looking after him in any systematic way. One day, he dashed out the screen door noshing on a piece of bologna rind. Horrified, I ran to give my Mother the blow by blow. What was it about that house and the rind of processed meats?

The first day they did the laundry and hung it on the clothesline, there was one grimy towel amongst the clothing. "Mom, my dear", I said. "How dirty are they at all? One towel for the hordes and masses in that house?" Surprisingly, they all seemed healthy and agile, albeit grungy. The lack of neatness and cleanliness (a WASPy Nipper's Harbour norm) meant there was lack of definition — they sort of all looked the same. The little boy was smaller than the others so he stood out a bit.

I learned a lot that summer. I wasn't the only one keeping close watch on those strangers, although nobody had the view I had. My theatre seat was the best seat in the house.

One day I overheard a woman telling my Mom that these neighbours had no curtains on their bedroom window, and there was a private giggle exchanged. By now I was old enough to know what was meant and felt quite sure it had something to do with the procreative potential of those heathen people.

But the usefulness of these neighbours was the experience of difference.

By the end of that summer I knew:

- Dirt itself will probably never kill you.

- Not everyone lived with the same norms I had grown up with in Nipper's Harbour.

- These people seemed happy enough. I never heard anyone fighting. Therefore, there must be more than one way to live.

- Although there was a growing tolerance for these folks over the summer, I still felt quite comfortable with my middle class life. There was no urge to embrace their lifestyle.

What a finale for my theatre seat. It was shortly after this episode that I went away to High School. It was good preparation for all the differences I would eventually see in my later career as a social worker.

Footpaths & Fishing Boats

Epilogue

The house was in the beach, with just a breakwater in front. It felt like the house was actually on the water, because when you looked out the kitchen window, that's what was immediately in front — the water, and wharves, and boats and breakwaters and seagulls and cliffs.

That's the kitchen where I used to wait with Nanc to go to school. The upstairs sunroom is where we spent many rainy days playing. The downstairs front porch is where sometimes the visiting nurse, Mrs. Gillespie, used to set up clinic and give us our inoculations.

That last summer, I slowed the car to a stop as I came down the hill. Nobody has lived in the house for many years. The windows have become undefined as the elements have stripped away the paint and edges. The old shop door is still there, and I can still hear Nanc's voice calling, "Me, Mom". I got out of the car and sucked in the salty sea air — it was a bombardment of sounds, smells and memories: Uncle Lo's long rubber boots scuffing on the pebble stones as he arrived home, the doorbell in the shop ringing as people went in and out on long summer days, the smell of bacon in the kitchen as Nanc noshed languidly on her toasted raspberry jam and bacon sandwiches before we left for school, and the warm tones of Aunt Alma's voice and Uncle Lo's twinkly face.

They don't know. The young people here now don't know the history of this wonderful house. What do they see when they look at this faded house on the beach? Do they know its rich hardwood floors have a story to tell? Can they imagine what it looks like inside?

In a phone call with my Mother a few weeks later, she said, "I heard they tore down Alma's house in the beach — flattened it." I felt a huge lurch in my stomach. Another tangible underpinning yanked from under me, leaving me to steady myself only with my memories, and the knowledge that some of the original people and homes still remained in Nipper' Harbour.

I then resolved that I would have to leave a written record of growing up in Nipper's Harbour, before Nipper's Harbour as I knew it physically disappeared.

It has been a struggle to let it go. This is what I have concluded: nobody can take away from you what your memory keeps for you. It's a fine place to keep in my heart. It was a fine place to grow up and they were fine people who made me who I am. I hope I am passing it on.

We have fine and great traditions, we
'the children of the sea'.

— E.R. Brown

Glossary

article rascal

bloomian blooming, bloomin', i.e. pesky

b'y boy

brewis (pronounced *brews*) hard tack is a sea-biscuit, made simply from flour and water. Because of its long shelf-life, and portability, it was used on sailing ships as a staple part of the diet. It requires soaking before being steamed or boiled and served with fish and salt pork scrunchions.

cod-trap (traps) a large three-dimensional stationary net optimally hauled up by two motorboats and a dory. This uses netting instead of hooks. The fish are alive in the trap and dipped out with a large **dip-net** after being concentrated by hauling up the netting.

flake (fish flake) an open platform for drying fish outdoors which allowed air circulation. A clap-board fish-cover was used to protect the collected fish in case of rain. Wind was desired for drying, since sunshine in still air could "cook" the fish.

keeled local dialect pronunciation of the word *killed*.

oakum loose fibrous material used to caulk boats to make them water tight.

oil clothes oil skins

render (render out) heating done by the sun would cause the oil to ooze out from the livers.

Room A water-front property, especially a commercial one, was called a Room.

stages (fishing stages) A small building extending out above the sea, used to process cod and other species for the market.

tawts (probably from thwart, athwart) boards running across the boat that were used for seating and other purposes.

tole (thole) thole pins were the vertical wooden pegs used instead of rowlocks.

trawls (trawl-lines) immensely long stationary lines which at regular intervals had short lines with baited hooks on which cod fish were caught.

Footpaths & Fishing Boats